British Grand Prix

at SILVERSTONE 1996

PHOTOGRAPH **JED LEICESTER**

CONGRATULATIONS JACQUES

THE WINNING FORMULA

WELCOME

from
Jacques Villeneuve

Since my team mate Damon Hill won my home race in Canada, it was satisfying to be able to turn the tables on him at his home Grand Prix at Silverstone.

It was a great feeling crossing the line in first place. I was very happy. After that first win, at the Grand Prix of Europe in April, we had some good results but most of the time it seemed we were second while Damon was doing the winning.

For the first time this season we were racing at a circuit I knew well from many laps of testing. This made it easier to become more aggressive quickly and I was determined to do that. A maximum effort was needed to fight with Damon, who had the bonus of the Silverstone crowd cheering him on and an even better knowledge of the circuit.

For his loyal British fans, and from the point of view of the team, it was unfortunate that Damon didn't finish the race. However, his failure to score points also made our battle for the Drivers' World Championship closer, and that factor made this win even more important than my first victory earlier in the season.

It's a race I will remember for a long time.

Jacques Villeneuve

PHOTOGRAPH **MARTYN ELFORD**

Editor Andy Hallbery

Designer Frances Kiernan

Picture editor Tim Wright

Sub editors Nick Carter, Andrew Benson

Photography AUTOSPORT PHOTOGRAPHIC: Martyn
Elford, Jeff Bloxham, Ralph Hardwick SUTTON
MOTORSPORT IMAGES: Keith Sutton, Mark
Sutton, Paul Sutton, Gavin Lawrence, Neil
Hepworth, Stuart Collins, Mark Leader, Alex
Littlewood, Mike Weston ADDITIONAL
PHOTOGRAPHY: Jed Leicester, Darren Heath,
Hugo Dixon, Mick Walker, Gary Hawkins,
Anton Want/Allsport Photographic, Jakob
Ebrey, Graeme Brown, Laurence Baker

Advertising & Publishing Manager Martin Nott

Production Guy Nicholls

Publisher Peter Foubister

Publishing Director Tony Schulp

British Grand Prix at Silverstone 1996
is published by Haymarket Specialist Motoring
Magazines, 38-42 Hampton Road, Teddington,
Middlesex, TW11 0JE England.
Tel 0181 943 5000 Fax 0181 943 5850

Printed in England by BR Hubbard Ltd,
Dronfield, Sheffield.

Colour origination by F1 Colour, Mitcham, Surrey.

Bound by JW Braithwaite & Son, Wolverhampton.

Distributed by D-Services, Leicester

A HAYMARKET PUBLICATION

Damon Hill

PHOTOGRAPH **MARTYN ELFORD**

CONTENTS

PHOTOGRAPHS **SUTTON MOTORSPORT IMAGES**

PHOTOGRAPHS **SUTTON MOTORSPORT IMAGES**

(bottom photo) **MARTYN ELFORD**

FIA FORMULA 1 WORLD CHAMPIONSHIP

10 - 13 July 1997 (provisional dates)

1997 British Grand Prix

Book now to secure your places for the 1997 British Grand Prix - the year's only appearance in the UK of the world's most glamorous sporting championship.

In 1997 the British Grand Prix meeting will be bigger than ever with the action now filling four days for the first time.

In view of exceptional demand in 1996, new and additional seating will be introduced for 1997 in a series of enclosures. But remember tickets will be limited to 90,000 per day.

- Sunday completely sold out in 1996 – in record time
- Buying a ticket in advance reduces pedestrian queuing and avoids disappointment
- Early bookers of centre transfer gain the opportunity to join in the Pit Road walkabout.
- Grandstand seats sold out 6 months prior to 1996 event!

To avoid disappointment...

Book now!

Use the official Advance Booking Form or call us on the Hotline:

01327 857273

Silverstone
THE HOME OF BRITISH MOTOR RACING

FOREWORD

by The Lord Hesketh

Welcome to this first annual of the greatest weekend in British motor sport – the British Grand Prix at Silverstone.

It goes without saying that staging the British Grand Prix is a monumental undertaking for Silverstone. Not only is it the most important event of the year at Silverstone, but for a world-wide audience, it is also a showcase for the whole of British motor sport, representing the best in technology and organisation.

The smooth running of the British Grand Prix is the result of the hard work and dedication of many individuals and companies over the weekend of the race, and many months before. This book brings in to focus the considerable efforts of the 5000 people who work at the Grand Prix behind the scenes, and the enjoyment of the 200,000 fans who come to Silverstone to be entertained by the superb eight-race programme. Our congratulations go to all the race winners, and particularly to Jacques Villeneuve in his first British Grand Prix.

I am delighted that Autosport has chosen to celebrate the British Grand Prix at Silverstone 1996 by publishing this book, and I hope you enjoy it.

The Lord Hesketh
PRESIDENT
British Racing Drivers' Club

PHOTOGRAPH **PAUL HOWARD PHOTOGRAPHY**

Man in a hurry: Jacques Villeneuve's faultless performance moved him into contention for the world title

PHOTOGRAPH **SUTTON MOTORSPORT IMAGES**

HEROES

by Adam Cooper

Twenty Grand Prix drivers lined up on the Silverstone grid. But there's no doubt that most fans came to give their support to one man – Damon Hill. Even the briefest survey of the banners in the spectator areas revealed that he was the focus of attention.

Hill came into the weekend leading the championship by 25 points, with six Grand Prix wins to his name thus far in 1996. Another victory on home ground would be an important step to the coveted title. And the fans knew it.

Damon, winner of this race two years ago, was pursued wherever he went. Constantly in demand for press interviews and sponsor appearances, he was under enormous pressure. While he enjoys the attention, at times it became too much. He overcame the first hurdle by securing pole position, and was probably quite relieved when he finally climbed aboard the car on Sunday afternoon, and the real action began.

Hill's race ended in disappointment, and when news of his demise came across on the track commentary, and the giant TV screens showed his Williams stuck firm in the Copse gravel, there was an audible groan from thousands of throats.

Michael Schumacher is perhaps not the most popular driver among British crowds, just as

Damon gets a tough time at Hockenheim, his rival's home patch. The German was himself already out, to the dismay of his visiting countrymen and the many Ferrari supporters. So the main beneficiary of Hill's demise was his team mate, Jacques Villeneuve.

This was his first motor race in Britain at any level, but the cool French-Canadian was already popular with the fans. Father Gilles, who made his F1 debut at Silverstone back in 1977, was an idol to many. If Damon couldn't win, JV was as good a back-up as any.

It's not just the drivers who are heroes. TV commentator Murray Walker is the voice of motor racing, and in Britain finds himself as swamped as Damon by enthusiastic well-wishers. This time, he received a special gift from the stars of the show – the drivers.

Then there are the thousands of folk involved behind the scenes, including the many volunteers who give up their weekend for the pleasure of being involved in a great sporting occasion. That includes the hundreds of course marshals and ambulancemen, whose services were barely needed over the course of a safe and efficiently run meeting.

They were heroes for a day.

Damon Hill is besieged by the world's media after taking pole position for his home Grand Prix

PHOTOGRAPH **SUTTON MOTORSPORT IMAGES**

A loose wheel nut sees the dreams of Damon Hill and the majority of the 90,000 spectators disappear into the gravel trap, his race over.

The exit of Damon Hill

PHOTOGRAPH **ALLSPORT**

To mark the occasion of the BBC's last British Grand Prix, World Champion Michael Schumacher presents the Corporation's legendary commentator, Murray Walker, with a magnum of champagne signed by all of the Grand Prix drivers. It was a touching moment, and one which displayed the affection the sport's stars have for the man who has done as much as anyone to make Grand Prix racing as popular in England as it is today.

Present for Murray

PHOTOGRAPH **MARTYN ELFORD**

12

Silverstone TV kept trackside spectators informed with action from on and off the track, interviews, reviews, and even traffic information. The images were broadcast to six giant screens and more than 2000 sets in the pit and hospitality enclosures, as well as the well-prepared race-goers with portable televisions. The 60-strong team included ITV's Dickie Davies, as well as F1's official commentator, Bob Constanduros, and the regular Silverstone team, led by Ian Titchmarsh and Paul Trusswell.

PHOTOGRAPH **SUTTON MOTORSPORT IMAGES**

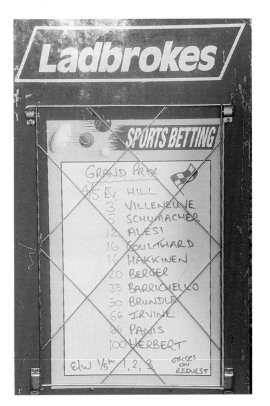

As well as being the fan's favourite, Damon Hill topped the betting odds throughout the Silverstone weekend.

Place your bets

PHOTOGRAPH **SUTTON MOTORSPORT IMAGES**

It may be 8pm on Saturday evening, but Damon still had time for the hoards of fans who had waited patiently for their hero to emerge

Damon in demand

PHOTOGRAPH **MARTYN ELFORD**

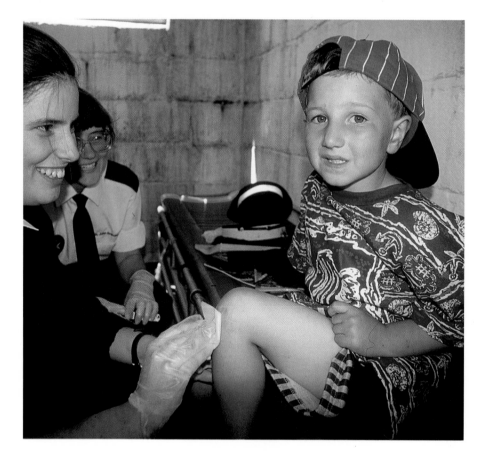

Safety is always a paramount concern for Silverstone, and the circuit has never stood still with its standards. This year there were 22 ambulance crews, four 'flying doctor' crews, and six rescue vehicle teams

FIA doctor, Prof Watkins

PHOTOGRAPH **MICK WALKER**

The medical staff are well-prepared. With 90,000 spectators, anything can happen

There, there… Now that doesn't hurt does it?

PHOTOGRAPH **LAURENCE BAKER**

Each pit garage is spotless, and must be kept that way. The McLaren mechanics set to work after David Coulthard made his mark…

'Perhaps we should try Flash?'

PHOTOGRAPH **JEFF BLOXHAM**

Villeneuve: centre of attention

PHOTOGRAPH **SUTTON MOTORSPORT IMAGES**

More than 700 volunteer marshals were on site, including 57 observers, 108 flag marshals, 30 incident officers and 325 fire and course marshals

The crew of HMS Stowe on parade

PHOTOGRAPH **JEFF BLOXHAM**

Scotsman David Leslie sped to Honda's first victory in the British Touring Car Championship

Honda – calm ahead of the storm

PHOTOGRAPH **SUTTON MOTORSPORT IMAGES**

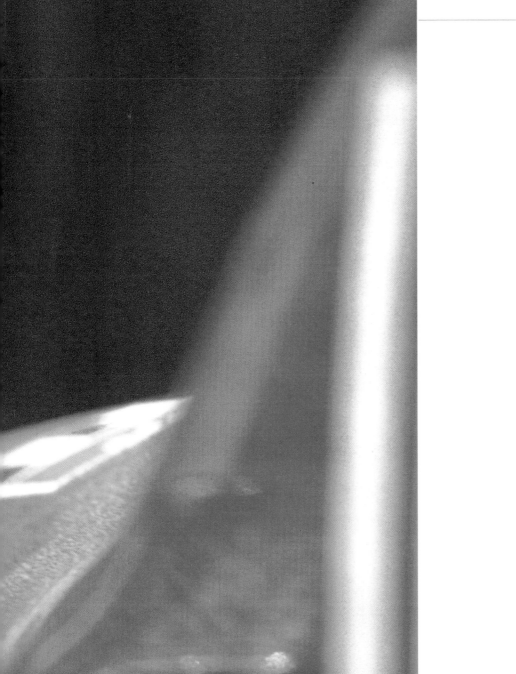

Michael Schumacher didn't need his mirrors for long on race day, the World Champion posting the first retirement. It was an extremely disappointing end for the German, who had taken the challenge to Williams during qualifying, holding provisional pole position for much of the first half of the session. It was a naturally spectacular on-the-limit lap, the scarlet machine darting from one side of the road to the other, riding high on the kerbs. Schumacher confirmed his commitment: 'I think I got the absolute maximum out of my car...'

Schumacher prepares to qualify

PHOTOGRAPH **MARTYN ELFORD**

Both McLaren–Mercedes finished in the points

PHOTOGRAPH **SUTTON MOTORSPORT IMAGES**

Hill and Schumacher provide some amusement

PHOTOGRAPH **RALPH HARDWICK**

The average person doesn't need a car with twin airbags and power steering.

The average person doesn't need a car with a high level brake light and a coded key pad immobiliser.

The average person doesn't need a car with electric front windows and three rear three-point safety belts.

The average person doesn't need a car with a driver's door mirror with built in blind spot eliminator.

The average person doesn't need a car with a six speaker remote control stereo radio cassette.

The average person doesn't need a car with a steering column with height and reach adjustment.

The average person has 2.4 children.

THERE'S NO SUCH THING AS AN AVERAGE PERSON.

THE NEW PEUGEOT 406 FROM £12,595.
FOR YOUR FREE INFORMATION PACK CALL 0345 000 406.

406
PEUGEOT

THE DRIVE OF YOUR LIFE

'When the flag drops, the bullshit stops'. An old adage that, unlike the starting procedure, hasn't been modernised

THE TEAMS

by Adam Cooper

Silverstone is but one stop on an eight-month world-wide trek for the Grand Prix teams. Commencing in Australia in March, and running through to Japan in October, they face a punishing schedule.

This year seemed tougher than ever, as from the start of the European season at the Nurburgring in April, there had been a constant rhythm of races every fortnight, with no three-week intervals to allow for a proper pause for breath. Since that German event, they'd been to Imola, Monaco, Barcelona, Montreal and Magny-Cours. With testing filling in most of the gaps between races, it's tiring for all concerned, not least the drivers themselves.

The July date may not have changed, but Silverstone was in fact the 10th of this year's 16 races, when it is usually the eighth or ninth. That partly explains why the paddock was abuzz with wild rumours about 'who goes where' for the following season. Usually such gossip doesn't get going until mid-August, but with the end of the season approaching faster than usual, many were already looking ahead.

For the British teams at least, Silverstone is a bit more relaxing than most European events.

The Williams, Benetton, McLaren, Jordan, Arrows and Tyrrell crews could take comfort in the fact that for once, there was no rush to the airport, no hanging around for delayed flights, no queuing for hire cars, no customs paperwork to be completed by the truckies.

For the Jordan team in particular it was a logistically hassle-free experience, since their base is just opposite the circuit's front gate. Of course, the downside is that everyone's friends and *their* friends want to get a free ticket and come along and visit. Saying no is not always easy...

For Ferrari, Ligier and the other continental outfits Silverstone requires extra effort. The crews come by plane, and the trucks make their way across on the channel ferries which through the summer months become so familiar to their British counterparts. Once at the track, they have to deal with the crowds and traffic jams. Mechanics are used to getting up early, but at Silverstone the 5am alarm call is particularly unwelcome. They also have to deal with the rule which forbids teams from testing at GP venues outside their countries.

Playing at home is more than just a psychological advantage.

The traditional chequered flag which the 11 F1 teams of 1996 strive to pass first

PHOTOGRAPH **SUTTON MOTORSPORT IMAGES**

FERRARI

On the British teams' home turf, Ferrari expected to have to play catch up, and the team had a troubled start on Friday, when Fiat boss Gianni Agnelli was present. Michael Schumacher claimed a respectable third when it mattered, in qualifying, behind the Williams duo. Following disasters in Montreal and Magny-Cours since Michael reigned in Spain, a good result was essential. He fell to fourth at the start, ahead of Hill. But on only the second lap he trailed into the pits stuck in sixth gear, the victim of a hydraulic failure. Eddie Irvine was left to hold the fort in a handy sixth place, but a few laps later an ominous cloud of smoke signalled his demise. After failing to start in 1994 and completing just three laps last year, the Ulsterman's Silverstone luck isn't getting any better. The spectacular smokescreen was caused by a transmission problem rather than an engine failure but, whatever the reason, the double retirement was a bitter blow for the beleaguered team, and particularly for boss Jean Todt.

Eddie Irvine RETIRED

PHOTOGRAPH **RALPH HARDWICK**

Irvine's Silverstone jinx struck on lap six this year...

PHOTOGRAPH **SUTTON MOTORSPORT IMAGES**

Michael Schumacher RETIRED

PHOTOGRAPH **MICK WALKER**

BENETTON

Gerhard Berger SECOND

PHOTOGRAPH **MARTYN ELFORD**

*Benetton-Renault drivers Jean Alesi and
Gerhard Berger enjoyed a competitive race
set-up, having had furrowed brows during
qualifying. Alesi held second place for the
first half of the race, but retired on lap 44
after a wheel bearing failed, leaving the
Frenchman enormously disappointed.
But in to his place came Berger, the
Austrian scoring his first podium finish of
the season having looked after his brakes
during an intelligent drive.*

LEFT

Jean Alesi RETIRED

PHOTOGRAPH **MARTYN ELFORD**

PHOTOGRAPH **SUTTON MOTORSPORT IMAGES**

WILLIAMS

Damon Hill RETIRED

PHOTOGRAPH **JEFF BLOXHAM**

Naturally, all eyes at Silverstone were on Damon Hill and the Williams team, and the World Championship leader did not disappoint his fans. He overcame a strong challenge from team mate Jacques Villeneuve to claim pole, leaving the Canadian frustrated after luck didn't go his way at one of the few F1 tracks he knows well. The tables were turned come the race; Hill made a bad start while Jacques led away, but we never got to see how their respective pit stop strategies would have panned out. Damon spun out at Copse after a front wheel nut worked loose, while Jacques continued on his untroubled way to take his second win of the season and, more importantly, reduce his team mate's championship lead to a fragile 15 points.

Jacques Villeneuve WINNER

PHOTOGRAPH **SUTTON MOTORSPORT IMAGES**

PHOTOGRAPH **SUTTON MOTORSPORT IMAGES**

McLAREN

McLaren had not been having the best of seasons but, after some promising results in the last tests before the Grand Prix, the team were hoping for a good run at home. Mika Hakkinen made the most of the latest updates to his car to qualify fourth, his best performance since his accident in Adelaide at the end of 1995. He made a great start to the race, comfortably holding off Hill, but ultimately his

Alain Prost McLAREN'S CHAMPION IN THE PIT LANE

PHOTOGRAPH **GARY HAWKINS**

Mika Hakkinen THIRD

PHOTOGRAPH **SUTTON MOTORSPORT IMAGES**

David Coulthard FIFTH

PHOTOGRAPH **MARTYN ELFORD**

two-stop strategy meant he could do nothing about the Benettons. But he was happy enough with third place, his first podium of the year. After starting only ninth, David Coulthard had a fight on his hands, but he managed to progress to fifth by the flag. But on this day, his Finnish team mate was in another class.

Pedro Diniz RETIRED

PHOTOGRAPH **MARTYN ELFORD**

LIGIER

Like the other overseas teams, Ligier was stymied by the lack of an opportunity to test at Silverstone. Nevertheless, qualifying positions of 16th (for Olivier Panis) and 17th (for Pedro Diniz) were extremely disappointing, especially as the French were celebrating Bastille Day on Sunday. Diniz made the better start and again impressed as he led his team mate early on, but shortly after a spin at Becketts he dropped out with engine failure. Panis – who sentationally won at Monaco earlier in the season – again showed that he is as good an overtaker as anyone in F1, but after several calls to the pits was forced to retire with handling problems. Not a happy weekend for him or the team.

Olivier Panis RETIRED

PHOTOGRAPH **JEFF BLOXHAM**

JORDAN

Jordan desperately needed to bag some points at Silverstone, their home circuit, after a few frustrating races. Qualifying went without major drama and Rubens Barrichello took sixth spot, while Martin Brundle showed he shouldn't be written off yet by taking eighth. A steady, consistent drive from Rubens earned him fourth place, while Brundle recovered from a mid-race puncture – which gave him a scary moment at Bridge corner – to scoop the final point. With both cars in the top six, Jordan could breathe a sigh of relief. It was time to party...

Rubens Barrichello FOURTH

PHOTOGRAPH **SUTTON MOTORSPORT IMAGES**

Martin Brundle SIXTH

PHOTOGRAPH **SUTTON MOTORSPORT IMAGES**

Michael Schumacher's understudy – in terms of German national pride – chose a one-stop race strategy to head home his team mate Herbert

Heinz-Harald Frentzen EIGHTH

PHOTOGRAPH **SUTTON MOTORSPORT IMAGES**

No surprise victory for Johnny Herbert this year...

PHOTOGRAPH **SUTTON MOTORSPORT IMAGES**

SAUBER

Heinz-Harald Frenzten has made a habit of qualifying in around 11th place this year, and there was no reason why Silverstone should be any different. Yet another team to spend time dialling into a circuit it doesn't test on, Sauber was in reasonable shape by Saturday when Frentzen took 11th (what else?), and local hero and '95 Silverstone winner Johnny Herbert was a couple of places behind. How could they progress from there? Opinions were divided. Johnny opted for two stops, HHF for just one. Alas, Herbert was caught behind his team mate at the start and could not take advantage of his lighter fuel load. He did eventually get past, but by the time the stop sequence sorted itself out, the German was ahead. Not that it mattered much – there's little difference between eighth and ninth places, which is where they ended up.

Johnny Herbert NINTH

PHOTOGRAPH **SUTTON MOTORSPORT IMAGES**

ARROWS

Silverstone may be the local track for TWR/Arrows, but budget restrictions meant they had little chance to take advantage of that. On the positive side Brian Hart had a new development of his V8 motor on hand, having finally introduced a pneumatic valve system. Still, Jos Verstappen could do no better than 15th with it. Team mate Ricardo Rosset, who had one of his best qualifying runs of the year, had the misfortune to be put to the back after inadvertently missing a weight check. At least that gave him the chance to pass a few people before he was stranded by an electrical problem. Meanwhile Verstappen gave the team heart (sorry...) by making it to the flag, albeit in tenth.

Jos Verstappen TENTH

PHOTOGRAPH **MARTYN ELFORD**

Jos Verstappen

'In qualifying we went the wrong way with the settings. We changed it back for the warm-up, and with 40 litres of fuel I was just two-tenths slower than my qualifying time… That's quite frustrating'

PHOTOGRAPH **SUTTON MOTORSPORT IMAGES**

Ricardo Rosset RETIRED

Ricardo Rosset and reflections of Rubens

PHOTOGRAPH **SUTTON MOTORSPORT IMAGES**

Ukyo Katayama RETIRED

PHOTOGRAPH **MARTYN ELFORD**

TYRRELL

It was 25 years since Jackie Stewart gave Tyrrell its most recent British GP win, and the chances of an anniversary repeat were considered slim, even by the most devoted of Uncle Ken's fans. Mechanical dramas restricted Tyrrell's lappery but, with confidence higher than of late, Ukyo Katayama qualified a strong 12th. Surprised to be beaten for once, Salo was a couple of places behind. Ukyo was in the thick of the midfield battle, but lost momentum when he had to take to the gravel to avoid a spinning Pedro Diniz. Shortly afterwards, Katayama's pit telemetry system lit up like a Christmas tree and he was told to stop. Mika was disappointingly far back early on in the race, but a good pit stop saw him leapfrog several cars and work his way up to seventh by the flag.

Mika Salo SEVENTH

PHOTOGRAPH **SUTTON MOTORSPORT IMAGES**

Pedro Lamy RETIRED

PHOTOGRAPH **JEFF BLOXHAM**

MINARDI

Giancarlo Fisichella ELEVENTH

PHOTOGRAPH **SUTTON MOTORSPORT IMAGES**

Fisichella and the Minardi team were always going to struggle at Silverstone

PHOTOGRAPH **MARTYN ELFORD**

Silverstone is not a circuit which rewards a nimble but seriously underpowered chassis and, without having tested there, the little Minardi team knew they would have trouble keeping up. Sure enough, Giancarlo Fisichella and Pedro Lamy were at the back throughout the weekend, until the penalised Rosset was put behind them on the grid. Lamy was an early casualty with gearbox dramas, but his young team mate plugged away at the back to record a finish in 11th and last place. At least they didn't run into each other, a feat they managed at Monte Carlo and Barcelona. And the motorhome pasta was as good as always.

FORTI

Forti's management spent Thursday and Friday trying to chase funds with which to ensure that Cosworth released its supply of engines. The cars emerged on Saturday afternoon to make a token attempt at qualifying, with a strict allowance of 9kg of fuel aboard. Suitably fired up with frustration, Andrea Montermini and Luca Badoer did but a couple of flying laps apiece before they ran out of gas and pulled off the circuit. The weekend's work over, the team packed up and made its way back to Italy...

First the cash ran out, then the fuel...

PHOTOGRAPH **SUTTON MOTORSPORT IMAGES**

Powerless: the Forti team sits it out

PHOTOGRAPH **JEFF BLOXHAM**

Andrea Montermini DID NOT QUALIFY

PHOTOGRAPH **SUTTON MOTORSPORT IMAGES**

Mercedes built the engine
Mobil built the oil

McLaren, one of the world's most successful Formula 1 teams and Mercedes-Benz, the maker of the world's most dependable road cars, rely on Mobil 1 engine oil.

Mercedes, renowned for their achievements in technical excellence, have developed a brand new V10 engine for the new McLaren MP4/11 Grand Prix car.

This 3 litre multi-valve engine produces more than 650 bhp at over 15,000 rpm powering the MP4/11 to a top speed over 330 kmh.

McLaren and Mercedes demand 100% reliability from every one of the 700 moving parts of the engine - including the engine oil.

They use Mobil 1 to protect the engine and keep it in peak condition through more than a million revolutions every Grand Prix.

Mobil 1 is an oil that will withstand internal engine stresses 8,500 times the force of gravity yet remains fluid and stable at temperatures which exceed 300°C. Mobil 1 is precision engineered to keep a film of lubricant between every moving part and virtually eliminate engine wear.

The Marlboro McLaren Mercedes Team trust Mobil 1, an oil that is also available for your car.

Whatever car you drive it's time you changed to Mobil 1.

It's liquid magic.

The world's most advanced engine oil

SMOKING CA

Chief Medic

6 mg Ta

MAKE LIGHT OF IT

Lights
BENSON *and* **HEDGES**

TOBACCO SERIOUSLY
DAMAGES HEALTH

USES CANCER

Officers' Warning
.6 mg Nicotine

Who says the fans can't get to the F1 drivers of today? Gerhard Berger signs away on Saturday evening

PHOTOGRAPH **MARTYN ELFORD**

THE FANS

by Andy Hallbery

The passion ran high. Support for Damon Hill was at fever pitch, with his white, blue and gold Williams cheered with a Mexican wave around every metre of the sweeps of Silverstone. His fans wore their T-shirts, hats, and jackets with pride, showing their allegiance to the World Championship leader. Others went to greater lengths to make their feelings about their favourite driver clear. Humorous and imaginative banners playing up the age-old England versus Germany battle, hundreds upon hundreds of union flags emblazoned with 'Damon Hill' across their centre, right up to painting their faces in the colours of the London Rowing Club just like their hero's crash helmet. This support was a big motivating factor for Damon, and he was quick to acknowledge the mass support in Saturday afternoon's pole position press conference: 'First of all I would like to thank all the fans for their tremendous support and encouragement. I really want to win for them, having achieved pole.'

Sadly, it was not to be. As his Williams slid into the gravel at Copse Corner, the mass groans from the terraces temporarily drowned out the sounds of the high-revving F1 engines.

But the British Grand Prix was not just about Damon Hill. Far from it. The spectators had their other favourites among the elite stars of the Grand Prix world, like the other home heroes; David Coulthard; Eddie Irvine; Martin Brundle; and 1995 British GP winner Johnny Herbert. Or Michael Schumacher, Jacques Villeneuve, Gerhard Berger or Jean Alesi. All were seen at the new Autograph Area at the back of the paddock, happily chatting and signing whatever was shoved in front of them. For the drivers it was a fleeting moment as they gave something back to the race-goers. For the fans, it probably made their weekend. These drivers *are* human after all...

The Marlboro unit in the spectator area was also something new, with Schumacher, Irvine, Hakkinen and Coulthard all being interviewed either on Friday or Saturday afternoon, after their team de-briefs had finished. Bringing the mountain to Muhammad was enormously popular with everyone, drawing massive crowds as can be seen from the photograph overleaf. Again, it was an initiative that brought the stars to the fans, and the response showed it was worth it. The message was very clear: It works!

No doubting who they support. But the question is, did they get the bus home like that?

PHOTOGRAPH **HUGO DIXON**

Michael Schumacher interviewed by John
Watson at the Marlboro unit

David 'Cardboard' and fan

PHOTOGRAPH **MARTYN ELFORD**

'Mini' Hakkinen is
out-numbered

PHOTOGRAPH **JEFF BLOXHAM**

The Damon Shop

PHOTOGRAPH **RALPH HARDWICK**

The famous five PHOTOGRAPH **JEFF BLOXHAM**

Michael Schumacher

'It doesn't matter which country we go to, I see the
different fans standing together and waving their flags in
support of different drivers. It can be different in other
sports, but in racing we have a good crowd behind us'

Euro '96 meets British Grand Prix

PHOTOGRAPH **SUTTON MOTORSPORT IMAGES**

*If Ascot has a tradition for outrageous headgear, then the British Grand Prix is most
definitely charging up on the rails*

A dedicated Jordan fan

PHOTOGRAPH **LAURENCE BAKER**

Not all visiting Germans were rooting for Schumacher…

PHOTOGRAPH **HUGO DIXON**

Cordon bleu in the Silverstone campsite

PHOTOGRAPH **RALPH HARDWICK**

Silverstone was alive with Damon Hill fever. While not quite approaching the 'Mansell Mania' of the early '90s, the patriotic ferver was tangible, making Damon's early exit from the Grand Prix all the more disappointing

Radio Silverstone on air

PHOTOGRAPH **RALPH HARDWICK**

PHOTOGRAPH MARTYN ELFORD

PHOTOGRAPH **SUTTON MOTORSPORT IMAGES**

There's no place like Silverstone at Grand Prix time for bringing out the sport-struck celebrities and 'beautiful
people'. Above, England rugby star Victor Ubogu shares a paddock joke with his companion; below (centre)
comic Vic Reeves gets to grips with the fiendish paddock turnstiles

PHOTOGRAPH **MARTYN ELFORD**

PHOTOGRAPH **MARTYN ELFORD**

PHOTOGRAPH **SUTTON MOTORSPORT IMAGES**

All the fun of the fair for those fans intent on living the Silverstone experience to the full. But they had to be careful not to spill their beer on the dodgems… The circuit funfair provided the perfect post-qualifying escape for visitors just too excited to take to their tents before Grand Prix day dawned

PHOTOGRAPHS **HUGO DIXON**

PHOTOGRAPH **SUTTON MOTORSPORT IMAGES**

Beatle and long-time Grand Prix fan George Harrison finds time for a pre-race chat with Mr and Mrs Hill. When George and Damon get together, discussions are just as likely to include guitar styles as they are the pit-stop strategy of the Williams-Renault team

The British drivers were much in demand…

Golfer Nick Faldo and son meet Damon Hill

PHOTOGRAPH **SUTTON MOTORSPORT IMAGES**

Labour leader Tony Blair with Damon PHOTOGRAPH **MARTYN ELFORD**

Eddie Irvine and Carl Fogarty PHOTOGRAPH **SUTTON MOTORSPORT IMAGES**

*The chance to meet up with old friends — and to make new ones — is
a big feature of the Silverstone Grand Prix for the British-based
teams, their drivers and families*

Mrs Hill with friend Lucy Boultwood

PHOTOGRAPH **MARTYN ELFORD**

Prince Michael of Kent and Patrick Head PHOTOGRAPH **MARTYN ELFORD**

Torvill and Dean meet Jonathan Palmer PHOTOGRAPH **SUTTON IMAGES**

The grandstands sold out well ahead of time

PHOTOGRAPH **SUTTON MOTORSPORT IMAGES**

Spectators try their hands at winning a Peugeot

PHOTOGRAPH **RALPH HARDWICK**

David Coulthard shares a moment with fans

PHOTOGRAPH **MARTYN ELFORD**

The carnival atmosphere stretched the length and breadth of Silverstone, with sponsor support teams offering chances to win all sorts of goodies and hundreds of trade stands selling thousands of items of F1 paraphernalia. And, if you knew where to look, you could spot the occasional star driver on a break away from the paddock

Titanium wheelnuts.
24ct gold heatshield.
Kenwood Hi-Fi.

The wheelnuts of the McLaren F1 supercar were specially machined from aircraft grade titanium to keep unsprung weight to an absolute minimum.

Pure gold was used as a heatshield in the engine compartment because it is, quite simply, the best material for reflecting heat.

And Kenwood were chosen to make an astoundingly light CD-autochanger that had to perform as well as the car itself.

Why?

Because the McLaren F1 was built without compromise. Totally.

KENWOOD

The sun rises over Silverstone, and everything is in place for the circuit's busiest day of the year.

COUNTDOWN

by Adam Cooper

It's no exaggeration to say that the build-up for the British GP starts the day after the previous year's race. The organisational challenge is huge...

Tickets go on sale straight away, and the administration department clicks into gear. This year there had been rebuilding work on the track during the winter, when Stowe corner was re-aligned. Of course, activity really gets going around April and May, when grandstands and hospitality suites are built and everything is repainted and made ready.

Through June and early July, the finishing touches are applied. On the weekend before the race, the first campers arrive, and the place is busy with contractors' trucks. The BBC's army of technicians lay cables and site the cameras which will capture the action for viewers worldwide.

The Grand Prix team motorhomes start to arrive in the paddock on Monday or Tuesday, and the first trucks, carrying their precious cargo of F1 cars, on Wednesday. The transporters are parked in perfect formation, all straight, and all polished. The teams also spend hours preparing their pit garages, making sure everything is in position, and spotless.

On Thursday the spectator campsites begin to fill up, and the volunteer officials, who've taken a couple of days off work to be at Silverstone, start to arrive. Arriving too are the F1 drivers, fresh from a few days break in their tax haven homes. The action gets underway on Friday morning as there are two days of practice and qualifying for the big event.

On Sunday morning the buzz comes from the helicopters, as thousands of VIPs try to beat the traffic jams. Outside on the A43 and the country lanes, the lines of cars edge towards the car parks, their occupants kept abreast of what's happening by Silverstone's own radio station.

At 9.30am the F1 cars have their warm-up, which is followed by a couple more support races. Most of the Grand Prix drivers are then required in the Paddock Club or other hospitality areas, meeting sponsors and talking through their weekend so far. From there it's the drivers' briefing and then the F1 drivers parade around the track, waving to the fans on the way.

Through lunchtime the tension builds, aided by the fearless Red Arrows, until the cars make their way to the grid at 1:30pm. Across five continents, millions tune in, ready for the British Grand Prix. And most are completely unaware of the 365 days of build-up...

The teams were on site five days prior to the race. Scrutineering takes place on Thursday

PHOTOGRAPH **SUTTON MOTORSPORT IMAGES**

Tyrrell built their pit on the Wednesday before the race, moving in their sponsor screens, computer equipment, tool trolleys and finally the Tyrrell-Yamahas themselves in a well-rehearsed routine. It's the same at all European races.

Tyrrell moves in

PHOTOGRAPHS **MARTYN ELFORD**

It's not just the engineering of the F1 cars that's millimetre perfect: so is the parking of the Grand Prix transporters. The FOCA TV mobile editing units – which control the on-board footage – take pride of place in front of the BRDC's brand new, and ultra-modern, race and control centre

PHOTOGRAPH **MARTYN ELFORD**

Holders of Paddock Club tickets make their way into the pit-lane for the Sunday Morning pit walkabout

Paddock Club pit-stop

PHOTOGRAPH **SUTTON MOTORSPORT IMAGES**

It's not just the Grand Prix drivers who are in demand in the hospitality areas. British Touring Car Champion John Cleland explains his tactics to the guests of the Autosport Tower on Sunday morning

'At the end of the straight, I turn right. .. I hope'

PHOTOGRAPH **LAURENCE BAKER**

More than 35,000 cars were parked on site at Silverstone on race day

'Now where did I leave my car?'

PHOTOGRAPH **SUTTON MOTORSPORT IMAGES**

The parade of nations

PHOTOGRAPH **SUTTON MOTORSPORT IMAGES**

The world's busiest airport – for a day

PHOTOGRAPH **SUTTON MOTORSPORT IMAGES**

On your marks, get set, go. The champagne area in the Paddock Club awaits the morning arrivals, while in a separate unit situated on the Hangar Straight, the tables are prepared for the 900 guests entertained by Jonathan Palmer's Promosport company. Sauber-Ford driver Johnny Herbert made an appearance on race morning

Champagne city

PHOTOGRAPH **RALPH HARDWICK**

Ladies and gentlemen, takes you seats for the main event

PHOTOGRAPH **JOHN COLLEY**

You've got to be able to see your face in it

PHOTOGRAPH **JEFF BLOXHAM**

Work continued day and night in the pits...

PHOTOGRAPH **JED LEICESTER**

...and in the kitchens

PHOTOGRAPH **SUTTON MOTORSPORT IMAGES**

'Oooh, isn't that Barrichello fella gorgeous...?'

PHOTOGRAPH **SUTTON MOTORSPORT IMAGES**

'Someone seems to have stolen Becketts...'

PHOTOGRAPH **SUTTON MOTORSPORT IMAGES**

Elevenses are interrupted by Eddie Jordan, Barrichello and Brundle

PHOTOGRAPHS **MARTYN ELFORD**

While the team mechanics worked tirelessly preparing their cars, or making sure that their transporters are prim and proper, nearly a quarter of the people at Silverstone on race day took part in the corporate hospitality packages. In the Paddock Club, which operates at every Grand Prix, guests could have their shoes shined, or even their hair styled by Vidal Sassoon's experts while quaffing the bubbly. Behind the scenes the thousands of crudités were prepared as drivers like Damon Hill, or the Jordan pair of Rubens Barrichello and Martin Brundle, gave the inside line on racing at Silverstone to the teams very special guests.

Among the many air displays on race morning was one from the
crack RAF Falcons Parachute team

Just dropping in

PHOTOGRAPH **SUTTON MOTORSPORT IMAGES**

On Friday afternoon, as part of their Grand Prix build-up, Virgin Radio broadcast the three-hour Nicky Horne Drivetime Show live from the Autosport Tower opposite the start finish line. Guests included McLaren-Mercedes star, David Coulthard.

Nicky Horne and David Coulthard

PHOTOGRAPH **MARTYN ELFORD**

PHOTOGRAPH **MARTYN ELFORD**

The 30 minutes prior to the start of the Grand Prix are when the tension rises to boiling point. All the cars must be in place 20 minutes prior to the start. The mechanics make their final checks while the drivers go into their special pre-race rituals. Some give live interviews to their home TV stations, while others stay sat in their cars, helmets on, trying to shut out the hustle and bustle surrounding them. With five minutes to go the grid is cleared, and pulses race. Then, with a burst of noise, the race is on.

Grid formation

PHOTOGRAPH **SUTTON MOTORSPORT IMAGES**

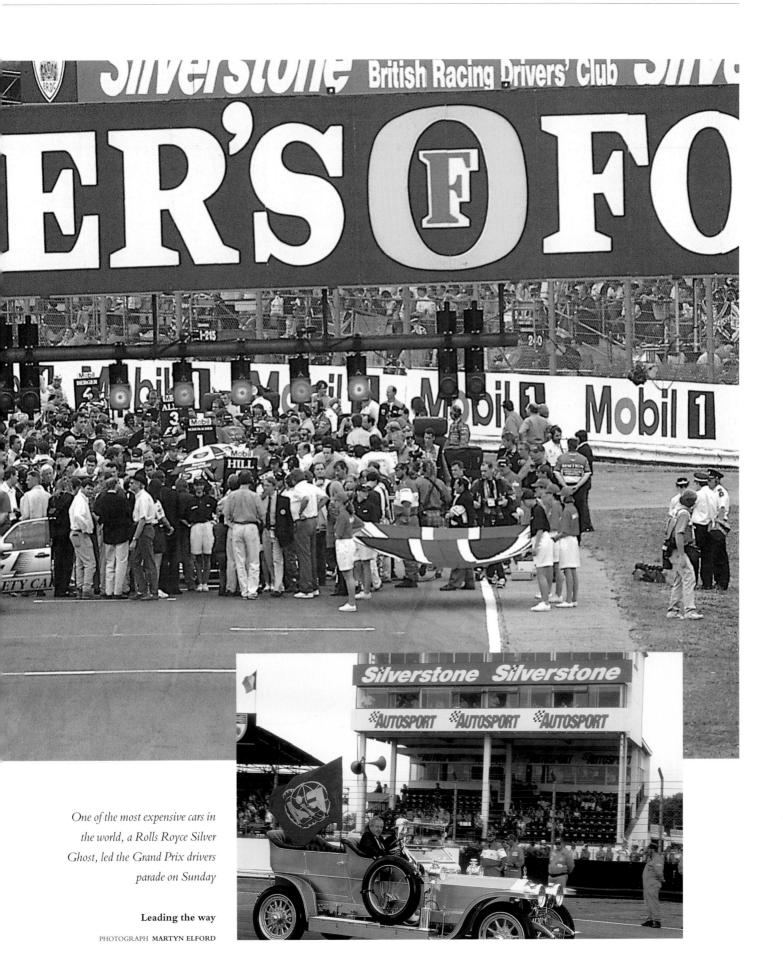

One of the most expensive cars in the world, a Rolls Royce Silver Ghost, led the Grand Prix drivers parade on Sunday

Leading the way

PHOTOGRAPH **MARTYN ELFORD**

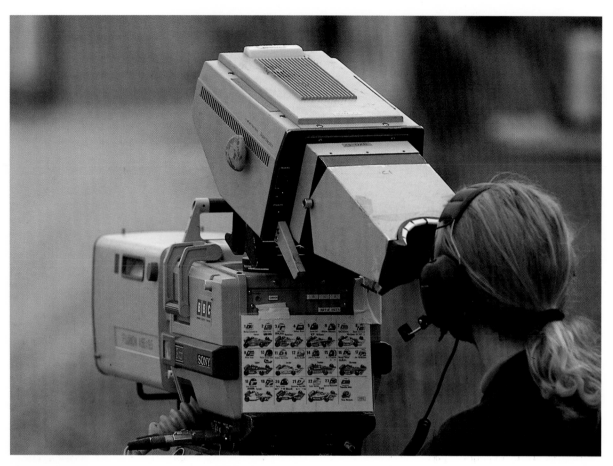

PHOTOGRAPH **RALPH HARDWICK**

The Grand Prix was relayed to the 90,000 spectators via Silverstone TV, and to the watching world via the BBC's host transmission. Information is of the essence and runners are employed to pass on news from the teams to the broadcasters as soon as it happens, whether it's official Formula 1 circuit commentator Bob Constanduros, or the BBC's very own Murray Walker.

Bob Constanduros

PHOTOGRAPH **SUTTON MOTORSPORT IMAGES**

OVER 30

BETTE[

ANY OT[

MORE F1 GRAND PRIX VICTORIES THAN AL[

O TIMES

R THAN

ER TYRE

THER TYRE MANUFACTURERS PUT TOGETHER.

FACT NOT FANTASY!

THE RACE

by Adam Cooper

Grand Prix racing is as much strategy as it is wheel-to-wheel action. All the elements must add up; pit-work is as vital as having a good race set-up; aggression must be tempered with care, drivers looking after the components to make sure of finishing. Shortly after 2pm on Sunday July 14, the five red lights went out to signal the start of the British Grand Prix. The cars set off on their 192-mile race journey.

The most memorable action in the British GP happened in the opening minutes. Having worked hard to secure pole, Damon Hill made a bad start and found himself passed by the Benetton-Renault of Jean Alesi and McLaren-Mercedes driver Mika Hakkinen. Alesi looked like he might take his Benetton all the way into the lead, but Jacques Villeneuve had the inside line for the first corner and wasn't about to let go.

Alesi slotted into second ahead of Hakkinen, Michael Schumacher and Hill. But on only the second lap the German's Ferrari slowed with transmission trouble; a few laps after that team-mate Eddie Irvine was out too. The attention focused on Hill and his efforts to pass Hakkinen, essential if he was to do anything about catching Alesi and Villeneuve. But before he could make his move, he spun off the road, the victim of a loose wheel nut.

After that, only an unexpected drama could rob Villeneuve, and there was none. However, he found himself with a different Benetton behind him after an angry Alesi struck brake trouble, handing second position to team mate Gerhard Berger. Hakkinen, having stopped twice for fuel and tyres maintained his pace on the way to third, ahead of the Jordan-Peugeot of Rubens Barrichello, David Coulthard's McLaren-Mercedes and the second Jordan of Martin Brundle, who'd been delayed during the race by a puncture.

Villeneuve, Berger and Hakkinen climbed the steps of the new BRDC control centre for the traditional victory ceremony, and the presentation of the 'Silver Magnum' to the race-winner.

Next stop, Hockenheim.

The sweet taste of success for Jacques Villeneuve

PHOTOGRAPH **RALPH HARDWICK**

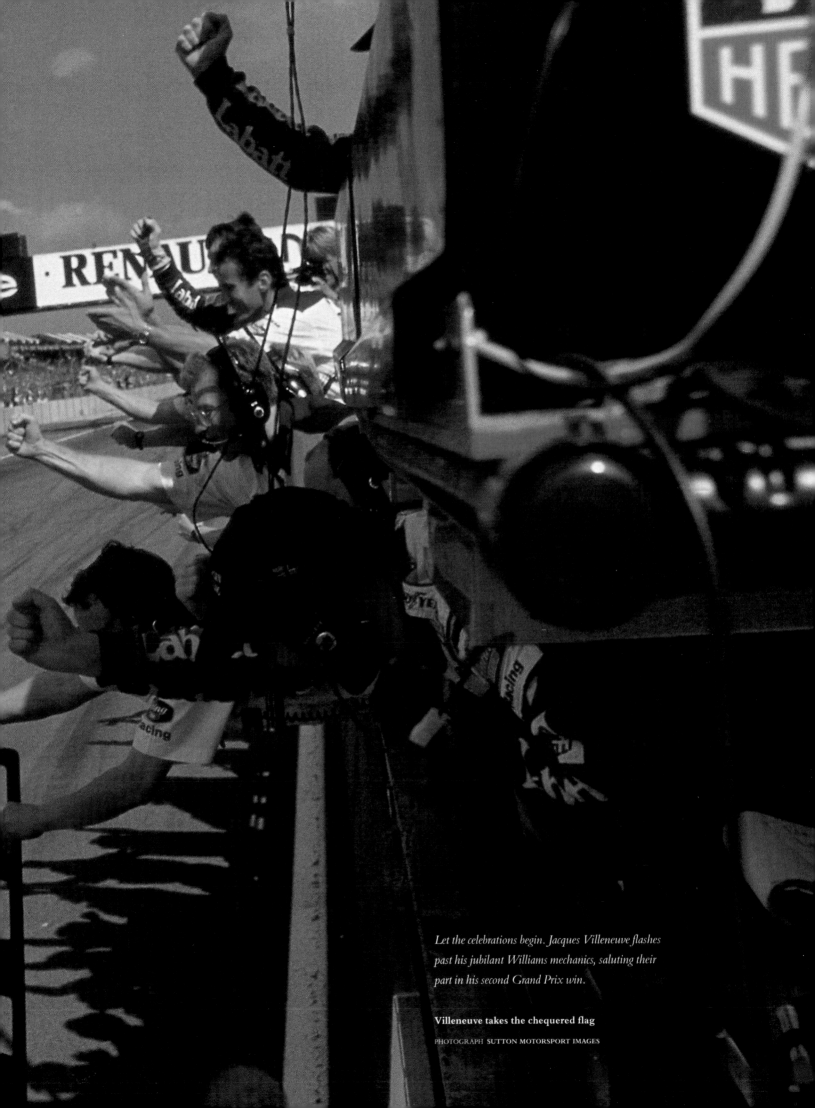

Let the celebrations begin. Jacques Villeneuve flashes past his jubilant Williams mechanics, saluting their part in his second Grand Prix win.

Villeneuve takes the chequered flag

PHOTOGRAPH SUTTON MOTORSPORT IMAGES

The start is all-important in F1, and Jacques Villeneuve knew that he had to beat Damon Hill on the run down to Copse

Corner. But Damon's start was not so good, and it was Jean Alesi who was hustling the French-Canadian.

'When I knew Damon had a bad start,' said Jacques, 'I didn't care why. I was just happy he had…'

Villeneuve leads the scramble to the first corner

PHOTOGRAPH **MARTYN ELFORD**

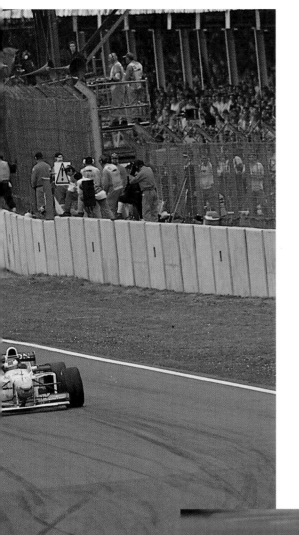

The Benetton pair both opted for single pit-stop strategies, having been further away from the pace of the Williams than expected during qualifying. In the second half of the race, Gerhard Berger caught up with Jean Alesi and engaged in one of the few on-track battles

Alesi and Berger – Benettons in battle

PHOTOGRAPH **RALPH HARDWICK**

David Coulthard was tenth at the end of the first lap, and fifth by the end of the race

PHOTOGRAPH **SUTTON MOTORSPORT IMAGES**

Overtaking! Berger passes Alesi

PHOTOGRAPH **RALPH HARDWICK**

Time to go home for Pedro Diniz

PHOTOGRAPH **RALPH HARDWICK**

Hakkinen heads Hill

PHOTOGRAPH **GARY HAWKINS**

If Ferrari had a weekend to forget at Silverstone, then the opposite could be said of McLaren and especially Mika Hakkinen. The Finn qualified fourth, and comfortably headed Damon Hill's Williams until the British driver's race ended in the Copse gravel on lap 26. McLaren's two-stop strategy was carried out to perfection, leaving Mika to complete the task, taking the flag in third place – his first podium finish since his terrible accident at Adelaide in 1995.

There was not much passing in the 1996 British Grand Prix, Ligier's Olivier Panis again proving to be one of those most on the move, before the Frenchman joined his team-mate, Pedro Diniz, in retirement. Home team Jordan had both cars finish in the points, Martin Brundle recovering from a puncture to take sixth place after a determined and aggressive drive. 'I'm back on form again,' Martin reported. 'Normal service is resumed!'

Pit-stop for third-placed Hakkinen

PHOTOGRAPH **SUTTON MOTORSPORT IMAGES**

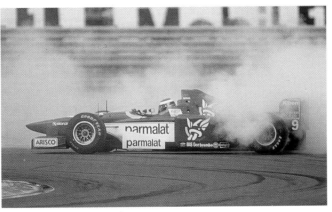

Panis suffered handling problems

PHOTOGRAPH **GRAEME BROWN**

Martin Brundle took sixth despite a puncture

PHOTOGRAPH **MARTYN ELFORD**

A despondent Michael Schumacher

*'This is absurd. Since the French Grand Prix we have tested at Monza and Imola and completed
two days of practice here at Silverstone all without failures. Now we come to the race, and we get this...
Still, in racing, things like this can happen.'*

PHOTOGRAPH **SUTTON MOTORSPORT IMAGES**

Schumacher retires on lap 3

PHOTOGRAPH **SUTTON MOTORSPORT IMAGES**

A dejected Damon Hill

'Naturally I was extremely disappointed when I got out of the car, but was relieved to be OK because the car had come off the track very fast. The disappointment of not winning descended swiftly. The support from the crowd had been fantastic all weekend, and they continued to cheer me as I walked back to the pits.'

PHOTOGRAPH **SUTTON MOTORSPORT IMAGES**

Game over, player one

PHOTOGRAPH **ALLSPORT**

The sweet taste of success also provides a sting in the eye for British Grand Prix winner, Jacques Villeneuve,
while runners-up Gerhard Berger and Mika Hakkinen trade bubbles on the winner's podium at Silverstone.

Champagne time

PHOTOGRAPH **MARTYN ELFORD**

AP Racing Competition Clutches are the standard by which all others are judged.

AP Racing offer a wider range, better design, dependable quality and unrivalled performance.

The results say it all - 123 Grand Prix wins for AP Racing Carbon / Carbon clutches alone *(our competitors only managed three between them!)* and our track record is equally impressive elsewhere.

Make contact with AP Racing for the ultimate in racing clutch technology.

THE INDUSTRY STANDARD

CARBON/CARBON ■ METALLIC 5¹/₂" ~7¹/₄" ■ SPECIAL TUNNING RANGE

Jacques Villeneuve punches the air in triumph as he wins the British Grand Prix

PHOTOGRAPH **MARTYN ELFORD**

THE WINNERS

by Adam Cooper

Silverstone winner Jacques Villeneuve has quickly got used to visiting the Grand Prix podium in 1996, although the British race was only the second time he's been on the top step. But he certainly wasn't the only winner in the course of an entertaining weekend of sport at the home of British motor racing.

The Auto Trader RAC British Touring Car Championship provided two entertaining races, one apiece on Saturday and Sunday. David Leslie caused a stir by putting his Honda Accord on pole for the first time for both of the the 15 lap races. Victory in the first went instead to Roberto Ravaglia and BMW, the Italian adding the win to a long list of career successes. Leslie got his revenge in the second race, and despite strong pressure from behind, held on in front to score Honda's first win in the highly competitive British series.

Some pretty famous names are to be found on the hall of fame of drivers having won the Formula 3 race supporting the British GP, including Ayrton Senna. To that list must now be added the name Speedsport Racing's Darren Manning, who held off Paul Stewart Racing team mates Ralph Firman Jr – the championship leader – and Jonny Kane.

The third single-seater race of the weekend was the Formula Renault Eurocup round. Brazilian Mario Haberfield was in a class of his own in a race notable for incidents and retirements – just 13 cars were running at the end.

The Porsche Supercup travels to most of the European GPs, and it was fitting that the race at Silverstone was won by a driver with F1 experience, albeit only in testing. Emmanuel Collard, Tyrrell's contracted test driver, scored his fourth win of the year against a field which included bike star Kevin Schwantz and former Formula 3000 ace Allan McNish.

The Renault Spider Eurocup is also seen at several GP meetings, and often the races are dominated by the Scandinavian contingent. This time Jason Plato won, followed by former Ligier F1 driver Frank Lagorce, and fastest lap was set by Williams test driver, Jean-Christophe Boullion. Finally, the Dunlop Rover Turbo Cup event was won by Alistair Lyall after a race which saw its fair share of pushing and shoving.

David Leslie celebrates winning Honda's first race in the British Touring Car Championship

PHOTOGRAPH **RALPH HARDWICK**

Jacques Villeneuve, British Grand Prix

PHOTOGRAPH **DARREN HEATH**

painted by J. MORLE

Roberto Ravaglia, Auto Trader RAC
British Touring Car Championship race one

PHOTOGRAPH **MARTYN ELFORD**

PHOTOGRAPH **JEFF BLOXHAM**

PHOTOGRAPH RALPH HARDWICK

David Leslie, Auto Trader RAC British
Touring Car Championship race two

Darren Manning, British Formula 3 Championship race

PHOTOGRAPH **MARTYN ELFORD**

PHOTOGRAPH **JEFF BLOXHAM**

Emmanuel Collard,

Porsche Pirelli Supercup race

PHOTOGRAPH JEFF BLOXHAM

Mario Haberfeld, Formula Renault Eurocup race

PHOTOGRAPH **RALPH HARDWICK**

Alastair Lyall, Dunlop Rover Turbo Cup race

PHOTOGRAPH JEFF BLOXHAM

Jason Plato, Renault Sport Spider Elf Trophy race

PHOTOGRAPH **JEFF BLOXHAM**

Hands on Power for Buying & Selling

Bike Trader -
Prime sponsors of the
British Motorcycle Race Day
at Silverstone
21st & 22nd September '96

The Perfect Racing Combination

Auto Trader -
Sponsors of
Alastair Lyall
& Nick Carr
in The
Dunlop Rover
Turbo Cup '96

Team Racing at it's Best

Auto Trader -
Official sponsors
of the
1996 Auto Trader
RAC Touring
Car Championship

Top Marques - The Best Cars

Nationwide choice for the discerning car
buyer - supporting the track day at
Coys International Historic Festival '96

The crowd is rocked by the traditional post-Grand Prix Jordan team party

PHOTOGRAPH **SUTTON MOTORSPORT IMAGES**

THE PARTY

by Adam Cooper

The British GP, perhaps more than any other Formula 1 race, is a time for partying. It's certainly the only event where a full-scale celebration is held in the paddock after the chequered flag, at a time when normally one would expect the regulars to be dashing for the airport.

During the weekend, many sponsors hold functions in the Silverstone area, and the drivers don team gear and make appearances, often in unusual locations. It's all part of the job. But the real action takes place at the track. Barbecues fizzle at motorhomes throughout the infield, and champagne glasses clink in the hospitality suites.

This year the race coincided with Bastille Day, so there was a special celebration among the French contingent. Renault held a function on Saturday evening, and all guests left with berets, a stick of bread and some camembert! Not to be left out, Peugeot had its own shindig on Sunday.

But as always, the event of the weekend was Eddie Jordan's post-race celebration, which has become something of a Silverstone tradition. Once the race was underway, a truck was driven across from his nearby factory to its allotted space in the middle of the F1 paddock. On it were set drums, microphones, amplifiers and all the other paraphernalia of a small-scale rock show. An hour or so after the touring car race finished, with the paddock bursting with people, the free concert got underway.

Changed out of his more familiar yellow and green outfit into a black T-shirt, EJ switched to his role as master of ceremonies and accomplished rabble rouser as he introduced the musical entertainment. Anchoring the beat was the group *Miss World* (anchored by former *Pretenders* drummer, Martin Chambers), joined at times by Eddie on a second set of drums. Other celebrities to make an appearance included *Pink Floyd* drummer Nick Mason and singers Haddaway and Chris de Burgh. Bravely stepping forth with only his guitar for accompaniment, de Burgh gave us The Lady in Red, and a few less familiar tunes.

The drivers always make guest appearances, and Johnny Herbert, Rubens Barrichello, Martin Brundle, David Coulthard and Mika Hakkinen were among those to get up on stage. As has become the norm, Herbert led the gang through an enthusiastic rendition of Johnny B Goode. Chuck Berry's job is not under threat yet.

Olivier Panis in patriotic mode, celebrating Bastille Day

PHOTOGRAPH **SUTTON MOTORSPORT IMAGES**

'I have my own drum kit and sometimes,' says Eddie Jordan, 'when I've had a really bad day at work, I come home, put on my earphones and play along. I know it drives the kids and the neighbours mad but I have to do it.' No danger of upsetting anyone at his team's Grand Prix party – except perhaps the odd music lover

Eddie Jordan drums up a Grand Prix party

PHOTOGRAPH **SUTTON MOTORSPORT IMAGES**

He promised to go on stage naked and sing Danny Boy if he won. He kept his kit on…

Martin Brundle, Jordan party

PHOTOGRAPH **RALPH HARDWICK**

Was he looking for the lady in red or hoping to see one of the red cars make it to the finish line?

Chris de Burgh, Jordan party

PHOTOGRAPH **RALPH HARDWICK**

A strange mix: In the musical corner, Pretenders drummer Martin Chambers and singer Haddaway. In the less
musical corner, Grand Prix racing's Supremes – Hakkinen, Brundle and Herbert

Haddaway and friends, Jordan party

PHOTOGRAPH **MARTYN ELFORD**

Spot the famous faces in the crowd at the Sunday night BTCC bunfight – a clue: some of the championship's accident-prone drivers are holding their beers aloft to prevent spillage. Top marks for getting Tim Harvey (far right), bonus points for other famous types

TOCA party

PHOTOGRAPH **RALPH HARDWICK**

*Even before race-day, the celebrities
(Dario Franchitti, left, and Tim
Harvey, far right) couldn't escape the
thrusting microphone of John
Hindhaugh from Radio Silverstone*

Pre-race parties

PHOTOGRAPHS **RALPH HARDWICK**

*The French couldn't let Bastille Day pass without a knees-up: the Renault staff and their countrymen sing the
Marseillaise to celebrate their national day. Not to mention a Renault 1-2 in the race!*

Bastille Day celebrations

PHOTOGRAPH **SUTTON MOTORSPORT IMAGES**

Publicly-relating PR people (from left) Jean-Jacques Delaruwiere of Renault, Vincent Franceschini of Tyrrell and Williams's redoubtable Annie Bradshaw indulge in some pre-GP horseplay

Renault Bastille Day celebrations

PHOTOGRAPH **EDGAR JESSOP**

Feeding the five thousand had nothing on this. But Jordan's caterers – like the team's engineers – are well used to achieving excellent results when the chips are down

Jordan party

PHOTOGRAPH **MARTYN ELFORD**

'David – you can take the balloon…' Mika Hakkinen pulls rank at the Mobil party to make a speedy exit,
leaving his team-mate with that up-in-the-air feeling

Mika Hakkinen, Mobil party

PHOTOGRAPH **ANTTI PUSKALA**

The party's over

PHOTOGRAPH **HUGO DIXON**

There's never been a dull Aston Martin

We're about to reveal our small, but significant, contribution to the glittering history of one of the most illustrious names in British motoring.

For nearly three decades, new Aston Martins have left Newport Pagnell with an Autoglym shine. If that comes as a surprise, then here's something else that may intrigue you.

Because of its service and special projects expertise, the Customer Service Division at Newport Pagnell attracts even not-so-new Aston Martins from all over the World. After receiving anything from a little tender loving care to a full restoration, they always leave with the added protection of Autoglym as a shining reminder of a classic tradition.

If you'd like to follow this fine example, you'll find a complete range of Autoglym's easy to use, car care products at all discerning car accessory shops.

Of course, you may not be fortunate enough to own an Aston Martin, but that's no reason why you should ever be seen driving a dull car.

BY APPOINTMENT TO
H.M. QUEEN ELIZABETH THE QUEEN MOTHER
SUPPLIER OF CAR CARE PRODUCTS
AUTOGLYM, LETCHWORTH, ENGLAND

BY APPOINTMENT TO
H.R.H. THE PRINCE OF WALES
SUPPLIER OF CAR CARE PRODUCTS
AUTOGLYM, LETCHWORTH, ENGLAND

AUTO GLYM

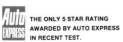

THE ONLY 5 STAR RATING
AWARDED BY AUTO EXPRESS
IN RECENT TEST.

AUTOGLYM, WORKS ROAD, LETCHWORTH, HERTS, SG6 1LU. TEL: 01462 677766 FAX: 677712

OVERSEAS DISTRIBUTORS: **AUSTRALIA** Crash Supplies Pty Ltd, Hornsby, NSW 2077 • **BELGIUM** S.P.R.L. Dejan, 8940 Wervik • **BRUNEI** Hock Hung Hing Auto Co, Darussalam
CANADA Autoglym Canada Ltd., Langley, British Columbia • **CYPRUS** A G P Trading Block Ltd, 6531 Larnaca • **DENMARK** S. Dyrup & Co. A/S, 5220 Odense SØ • **FINLAND** Autokem Oy, 36200 Kangasala
FRANCE CECM Distribution, 78630 Orgeval • **GERMANY** in process of change • **GREECE** Auto Decor, Athens • **HOLLAND** Handelmij H.M.S.b.v., 3860 AH Nijkerk • **HONG KONG** Dah Chon Hong (MSC) Ltd, Ap Lei Chau
INDONESIA PT Piramida Catur Pratama, Jakarta 12140 • **IRELAND** (Republic) Jay Agencies, Co. Dublin • **ISRAEL** J Jacobi & Sons, 66522 Tel Aviv • **ITALY** Sherwood s.r.l., Reggio Emilia • **JAPAN** Technoil Japon KK, Tsuzuki-Ku Yokohama
MALAYSIA Syarikat Kit Loong Sdn Bhd, Selangor • **MALTA** A W Said, Birkirkara • **MAURITIUS** Allied Motors Co.Ltd., Port Louis • **NORWAY** Krefting & Co AS, 1344 Haslum • **SINGAPORE** Sinamex Marketing Pte Ltd, Singapore 0207
SAUDI ARABIA Swayeh Co, Riyadh 11451 • **SOUTH AFRICA** Osmac, Johannesburg • **SPAIN** Autobrillante S.A. Madrid • **SRI LANKA** Consolidated Agencies (Pvt.) Ltd., Colombo 02 • **SWEDEN** IFC Willco Kemi AB, S-260 35 Odakra
TAIWAN Ho Jeh Enterprises Co Ltd., Taipei • **THAILAND** Kas Glym Int Co Lt., Bankok 10110 USA Motor Car Valet Inc., Utah 84121 • **URUGUAY** Estacion Independencia S.R.L., Montevideo • **WEST INDIES** TKK Auto Services Ltd., Trinidad

The 900 guests in the Jonathan Palmer Grand Prix Scene are kept up to date with the F1 action

PHOTOGRAPH **JOHN COLLEY**

FACTS

by Nick Carter

For just over 90 minutes on Sunday July 14, 1996, the eyes of millions of people around the world were focused on Silverstone, and the drama of the British Grand Prix. The watching world could be forgiven for believing that the race was simply a matter of 20 men and their machines battling over 61 laps of the Northamptonshire circuit. The reality is very different, and the numbers of people involved quite staggering.

For behind each Formula 1 driver is a team of mechanics, engineers, technicians, tacticians, computer boffins, media people, sponsor hunters, cooks and bottle-washers. A veritable army, without whom no Grand Prix car – nor, for that matter, any of the 150-plus cars in the seven supporting races – would move so much as out of the pit lane.

But the people who make the cars run are but a fraction of the bigger picture. Staging an event such as the British Grand Prix requires legions of – largely unpaid – staff, like the thousand-plus volunteer marshals who risk life and limb to be close to the sport they love, and be part of a great British sporting occasion.

Over Grand Prix weekend, Silverstone became the biggest employer in the region to cope with the 200,000-plus crowd who visited the circuit over the three days. The caterers alone hired 1800 temporary staff, and hundreds more helpers were needed to guide the 35,000 spectators' cars into and out of the car parks.

Silverstone also annually becomes the busiest airport in the world, with more than 3500 take-offs and landings on Grand Prix day alone... *Apocalypse Now* is nothing compared to the chattering choppers that wake the campers.

The facts flow freely: Silverstone installed 458 extra power sockets over GP weekend; around 1000 two-way radios were used on site; 44 PA systems were in operation; more than 22,000 three-course meals were served; an area of 250,000 square feet was covered by marquees supplied by Owen Brown; in excess of 700 telephone lines were in use (not counting the thousands of mobile phones present); 485 TVs were installed...

Overleaf you can find further facts and figures – the results and data from the Grand Prix itself (thanks to the wizardry of the Tag Heuer timing system) and all the support races, timed by MST.

Laps are timed to the 1000th of a second. Ricardo Rosset studies qualifying

PHOTOGRAPH **MARTYN ELFORD**

BRITISH GRAND PRIX FREE PRACTICE TIMES

POSITION	DRIVER	NAT	CAR	FREE PRACTICE	WARM-UP
1	DAMON HILL	GBR	WILLIAMS-RENAULT FW18	1m 26.560s	1m 29.696s
2	JACQUES VILLENEUVE	CAN	WILLIAMS-RENAULT FW18	1m 27.028s	1m 29.093s
3	MICHAEL SCHUMACHER	GER	FERRARI F310	1m 27.624s	1m 29.889s
4	RUBENS BARRICHELLO	BRA	JORDAN-PEUGEOT 196	1m 27.705s	1m 30.598s
5	GERHARD BERGER	AUT	BENETTON-RENAULT B196	1m 27.996s	1m 30.604s
6	MIKA HAKKINEN	FIN	McLAREN-MERCEDES MP4/11	1m 28.013s	1m 28.993s
7	JEAN ALESI	FRA	BENETTON-RENAULT B196	1m 28.364s	1m 29.893s
8	MARTIN BRUNDLE	GBR	JORDAN-PEUGEOT 196	1m 28.384s	1m 30.201s
9	DAVID COULTHARD	GBR	McLAREN-MERCEDES MP4/11	1m 28.417s	1m 31.610s
10	EDDIE IRVINE	GBR	FERRARI F310	1m 29.182s	1m 30.268s
11	OLIVIER PANIS	FRA	LIGIER-MUGEN HONDA JS43	1m 29.236s	1m 30.206s
12	HEINZ-HARALD FRENTZEN	GER	SAUBER-FORD C15	1m 29.312s	1m 31.222s
13	JOHNNY HERBERT	GBR	SAUBER-FORD C15	1m 29.549s	1m 30.400s
14	JOS VERSTAPPEN	NED	FOOTWORK-HART FA17	1m 29.684s	1m 30.308s
15	UKYO KATAYAMA	JAP	TYRRELL-YAMAHA 024	1m 29.777s	1m 31.522s
16	MIKA SALO	FIN	TYRRELL-YAMAHA 024	1m 29.810s	1m 32.292s
17	PEDRO DINIZ	BRA	LIGIER-MUGEN HONDA JS43	1m 30.743s	1m 31.491s
18	RICARDO ROSSET	BRA	FOOTWORK-HART FA17	1m 31.032s	1m 33.355s
19	GIANCARLO FISICHELLA	ITA	MINARDI-FORD M196	1m 31.450s	1m 33.204s
20	PEDRO LAMY	POR	MINARDI-FORD M196	1m 31.661s	1m 33.103s
–	LUCA BADOER	ITA	FORTI-FORD FG-03	No time	—
–	ANDREA MONTERMINI	ITA	FORTI-FORD FG-03	No time	—

PHOTOGRAPH **MARTYN ELFORD**   PHOTOGRAPH **JEFF BLOXHAM**   PHOTOGRAPHS **SUTTON MOTORSPORT IMAGES**

Ready for action • Schumacher checks the times • Hill gets ready to go • Forti mechanics wait for engines

The future of motorsport racewear...

...has arrived.

GRAND PRIX RACEWEAR

Incorporating ROAD & RACING ACCESSORIES

POWER ROAD • CHISWICK • LONDON W4 5PY • TEL: 0181 742 8000 • FAX: 0181 742 8999
email: racewear@grandpri.demon.co.uk web: http://www.grandpri.co.uk

FORMULA 1 WORLD CHAMPIONSHIP

POSITION	DRIVER	NAT	CAR	TIME	MPH
1	DAMON HILL	GBR	WILLIAMS-RENAULT FW18	1m 26.875s	130.583
2	JACQUES VILLENEUVE	CAN	WILLIAMS-RENAULT FW18	1m 27.070s	130.291
3	MICHAEL SCHUMACHER	GER	FERRARI F310	1m 27.707s	129.345
4	MIKA HAKKINEN	FIN	McLAREN-MERCEDES MP4/11	1m 27.856s	129.125
5	JEAN ALESI	FRA	BENETTON-RENAULT B196	1m 28.307s	128.466
6	RUBENS BARRICHELLO	BRA	JORDAN-PEUGEOT 196	1m 28.409s	128.318
7	GERHARD BERGER	AUT	BENETTON-RENAULT B196	1m 28.653s	127.964
8	MARTIN BRUNDLE	GBR	JORDAN-PEUGEOT 196	1m 28.946s	127.543
9	DAVID COULTHARD	GBR	McLAREN-MERCEDES MP4/11	1m 28.966s	127.514
10	EDDIE IRVINE	GBR	FERRARI F310	1m 29.186s	127.199
11	HEINZ-HARALD FRENTZEN	GER	SAUBER-FORD C15	1m 29.591s	126.625
12	UKYO KATAYAMA	JAP	TYRRELL-YAMAHA 024	1m 29.913s	126.171
13	JOHNNY HERBERT	GBR	SAUBER-FORD C15	1m 29.947s	126.123
14	MIKA SALO	FIN	TYRRELL-YAMAHA 024	1m 29.949s	126.121
15	JOS VERSTAPPEN	NED	FOOTWORK-HART FA17	1m 30.102s	125.906
16	OLIVIER PANIS	FRA	LIGIER-MUGEN HONDA JS43	1m 30.167s	125.816
17	PEDRO DINIZ	BRA	LIGIER-MUGEN HONDA JS43	1m 31.076s	124.560
18	GIANCARLO FISICHELLA	ITA	MINARDI-FORD M196	1m 31.365s	124.166
19	PEDRO LAMY	POR	MINARDI-FORD M196	1m 31.454s	124.045
20	RICARDO ROSSET	BRA	FOOTWORK-HART FA17	Time disallowed	—
DNQ	ANDREA MONTERMINI	ITA	FORTI-FORD FG-03	1m 35.206s	119.157
DNQ	LUCA BADOER	ITA	FORTI-FORD FG-03	1m 35.304s	119.034

BRITISH GRAND PRIX QUALIFYING

PHOTOGRAPH **MICK WALKER**

PHOTOGRAPH **MARTYN ELFORD**

PHOTOGRAPH **MICK WALKER**

PHOTOGRAPH **MARTYN ELFORD**

Ron Dennis waits for Hakkinen • Barrichello leaves the pits • Irvine studies form • Hill shares pole position with the crowd

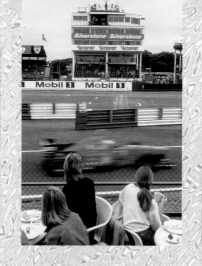

Gilmour & Pether

Official caterers to The British Grand Prix at Silverstone

The British Grand Prix is the largest single day event in the UK with over 2,000 catering staff ensuring that over 18,000 hospitality guests are served in the space of two hours.

Creative, flexible and affordable, Gilmour and Pether are dedicated to make your event a success at any venue for any numbers.

CHA
CORPORATE HOSPITALITY AND EVENT ASSOCIATION
CATERER OF THE YEAR

For further information contact:
PATRICK GILMOUR or DAVID PETHER
Tel: 01280 701 611
Fax: 01280 701 251

Gilmour & Pether

ONE OF THE HALLMARKS OF GARDNER MERCHANT LEISURE

			BRITISH GRAND PRIX			
POSITION	DRIVER	NAT	CAR	LAPS	TIME/REASON	MPH
1	JACQUES VILLENEUVE	CAN	WILLIAMS-RENAULT FW18	61	1h 33m 00.874s	123.997
2	GERHARD BERGER	AUT	BENETTON-RENAULT B196	61	1h 33m 19.900s	123.575
3	MIKA HAKKINEN	FIN	MCLAREN-MERCEDES MP4/11	61	1h 33m 51.704s	122.878
4	RUBENS BARRICHELLO	BRA	JORDAN-PEUGEOT 196	61	1h 34m 07.590s	122.531
5	DAVID COULTHARD	GBR	MCLAREN-MERCEDES MP4/11	61	1h 34m 23.381s	122.190
6	MARTIN BRUNDLE	GBR	JORDAN-PEUGEOT 196	60	1h 33m 17.786s	121.595
7	MIKA SALO	FIN	TYRRELL-YAMAHA 024	60	1h 33m 38.262s	121.152
8	HEINZ-HARALD FRENTZEN	GER	SAUBER-FORD C15	60	1h 33m 59.701s	120.692
9	JOHNNY HERBERT	GBR	SAUBER-FORD C15	60	1h 34m 00.496s	120.674
10	JOS VERSTAPPEN	NED	FOOTWORK-HART FA17	60	1h 34m 05.550s	120.566
11	GIANCARLO FISICHELLA	ITA	MINARDI-FORD M196	59	1h 34m 04.161s	118.586
R	JEAN ALESI	FRA	BENETTON-RENAULT B196	44	BRAKES	
R	OLIVIER PANIS	FRA	LIGIER-MUGEN HONDA JS43	40	HANDLING	
R	PEDRO DINIZ	BRA	LIGIER-MUGEN HONDA JS43	38	ENGINE	
R	DAMON HILL	GBR	WILLIAMS-RENAULT FW18	26	LOOSE WHEELNUT	
R	PEDRO LAMY	POR	MINARDI-FORD M196	21	GEAR SELECTION	
R	RICARDO ROSSET	BRA	FOOTWORK-HART FA17	13	ELECTRICS	
R	UKYO KATAYAMA	JAP	TYRRELL-YAMAHA 024	12	ENGINE	
R	EDDIE IRVINE	GBR	FERRARI F310	5	DIFFERENTIAL	
R	MICHAEL SCHUMACHER	GBR	FERRARI F310	3	GEARBOX HYDRAULICS	
FASTEST LAP		**JACQUES VILLENEUVE**			**1m 29.288s**	**127.054**

PHOTOGRAPH **MARTYN ELFORD**

PHOTOGRAPH **MARTYN ELFORD**

PHOTOGRAPH **GARY HAWKINS**

PHOTOGRAPH **MARTYN ELFORD**

Berger explains his race • Alesi retires • Brundle before the start • Villeneuve celebrates with his team

	AUTO TRADER RAC TOURING CAR CHAMPIONSHIP – ROUND 15					
POSITION	**DRIVER**	**NAT**	**CAR**	**LAPS**	**TIME/REASON**	**MPH**
1	ROBERTO RAVAGLIA	ITA	BMW 320i	15	30m 01.86s	94.46
2	RICKARD RYDELL	SWE	VOLVO 850	15	30m 02.05s	94.45
3	FRANK BIELA	GER	AUDI A4	15	30m 03.37s	94.38
4	DAVID LESLIE	GBR	HONDA ACCORD	15	30m 04.17s	94.34
5	JOACHIM WINKELHOCK	GER	BMW 320i	15	30m 04.85s	94.30
6	ALAIN MENU	SWI	RENAULT LAGUNA	15	30m 05.90s	94.25
7	KELVIN BURT	GBR	VOLVO 850	15	30m 12.19s	93.92
8	JAMES THOMPSON	GBR	VAUXHALL VECTRA	15	30m 15.73s	93.74
9	WILL HOY	GBR	RENAULT LAGUNA	15	30m 17.27s	93.66
10	JOHN CLELAND	GBR	VAUXHALL VECTRA	15	30m 21.70s	93.43
11	JOHN BINTCLIFFE	GBR	AUDI A4	15	30m 35.16s	92.74
12	RICHARD KAYE	GBR	VAUXHALL CAVALIER	15	30m 36.77s	92.66
13	GARY AYLES	GBR	NISSAN PRIMERA	15	30m 53.84s	91.81
14	LEE BROOKES	GBR	TOYOTA CARINA E	15	31m 07.24s	91.15
R	ROBB GRAVETT	GBR	FORD MONDEO	11	WHEEL BEARING	
R	OWEN McAULEY	GBR	NISSAN PRIMERA	10	ACCIDENT	
R	TIM HARVEY	GBR	PEUGEOT 406	9	ACCIDENT DAMAGE	
R	PAUL RADISICH	NZ	FORD MONDEO	9	ACCIDENT DAMAGE	
R	JAMES KAYE	GBR	HONDA ACCORD	7	FUEL RAIL	
R	STEVE ROBERTSON	GBR	FORD MONDEO	5	ACCIDENT DAMAGE	
R	PATRICK WATTS	GBR	PEUGEOT 406	2	ENGINE	
R	MATT NEAL	GBR	FORD MONDEO	1	ENGINE	
FASTEST LAP FRANK BIELA					**1m 58.57s**	**95.70**

UNISYS

PHOTOGRAPH **SUTTON IMAGES**   PHOTOGRAPH **GARY HAWKINS**   PHOTOGRAPH **LAURENCE BAKER**   PHOTOGRAPH **SUTTON IMAGES**

Championship leader Frank Biela • The Volvo cockpit • Rickard Rydell shares a joke with John Cleland • Young guns Burt and Thompson

POSITION	DRIVER	NAT	CAR	LAPS	TIME/REASON	MPH
AUTO TRADER RAC TOURING CAR CHAMPIONSHIP – ROUND 16						
1	DAVID LESLIE	GBR	HONDA ACCORD	15	29m 56.27s	94.75
2	FRANK BIELA	GER	AUDI A4	15	29m 57.15s	94.70
3	ROBERTO RAVAGLIA	ITA	BMW 320i	15	29m 57.63s	94.68
4	RICKARD RYDELL	SWE	VOLVO 850	15	29m 58.08s	94.66
5	ALAIN MENU	SWI	RENAULT LAGUNA	15	30m 00.94s	94.51
6	WILL HOY	GBR	RENAULT LAGUNA	15	30m 18.95s	93.57
7	JAMES THOMPSON	GBR	VAUXHALL VECTRA	15	30m 19.43s	93.55
8	KELVIN BURT	GBR	VOLVO 850	15	30m 20.11s	93.51
9	PAUL RADISICH	NZ	FORD MONDEO	15	30m 20.96s	93.47
10	JOHN BINTCLIFFE	GBR	AUDI A4	15	30m 21.62s	93.43
11	JAMES KAYE	GBR	HONDA ACCORD	15	30m 33.84s	92.81
12	STEVE ROBERTSON	GBR	FORD MONDEO	15	30m 35.52s	92.73
13	TIM HARVEY	GBR	PEUGEOT 406	15	30m 43.05s	92.35
14	RICHARD KAYE	GBR	VAUXHALL CAVALIER	15	30m 44.03s	92.30
15	GARY AYLES	GBR	NISSAN PRIMERA	15	30m 50.39s	91.98
16	LEE BROOKES	GBR	TOYOTA CARINA E	15	30m 58.43s	91.58
17	MATT NEAL	GBR	FORD MONDEO	15	31m 02.17s	91.40
18	ROBB GRAVETT	GBR	FORD MONDEO	12	31m 27.88s	72.12
R	JOACHIM WINKELHOCK	GER	BMW 320i	10	PUNCTURE	
R	JOHN CLELAND	GBR	VAUXHALL VECTRA	1	ACCIDENT DAMAGE	
R	PATRICK WATTS	GBR	PEUGEOT 406	0	ACCIDENT DAMAGE	
R	OWEN McAULEY	GBR	NISSAN PRIMERA	0	DRIVESHAFT	
FASTEST LAP RICKARD RYDELL					**1m 58.71s**	**95.58**

 UNISYS

PHOTOGRAPH **JEFF BLOXHAM**   PHOTOGRAPH **JEFF BLOXHAM**   PHOTOGRAPH **GRAEME BROWN**   PHOTOGRAPH **MARTYN ELFORD**

Radisich takes to the grass • The winner's autograph • Cleland on the kerbs • The sun shines on Ravaglia's BMW

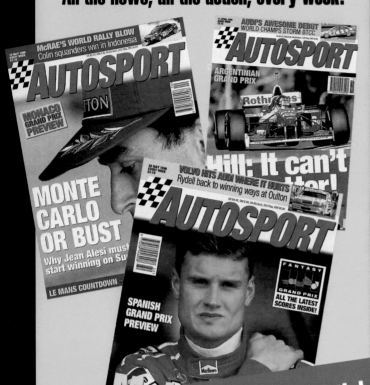

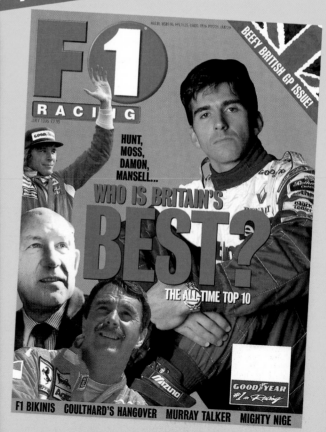

	BRITISH FORMULA 3 CHAMPIONSHIP					
POSITION	DRIVER	NAT	CAR	LAPS	TIME/REASON	MPH
1	DARREN MANNING	GBR	DALLARA F396 MUGEN	15	27m 24.08s	103.52
2	RALPH FIRMAN	GBR	DALLARA F396 MUGEN	15	27m 24.81s	103.48
3	JONNY KANE	GBR	DALLARA F396 MUGEN	15	27m 25.10s	103.46
4	KURT MOLLEKENS	BEL	DALLARA F396 MUGEN	15	27m 25.71s	103.42
5	BRIAN CUNNINGHAM	USA	DALLARA F396 MUGEN	15	27m 31.82s	103.04
6	GUY SMITH	GBR	DALLARA F396 MITSUBISHI	15	27m 38.28s	102.64
7	JUAN PABLO MONTOYA	COL	DALLARA F396 MITSUBISHI	15	27m 39.14s	102.58
8	BRIAN SMITH	ARG	TOM'S 036F TOYOTA	15	27m 39.97s	102.53
9	NICOLAS MINASSIAN	FRA	DALLARA F396 RENAULT	15	27m 40.89s	102.48
10	JAMES MATTHEWS	GBR	DALLARA F396 RENAULT	15	27m 41.76s	102.42
11	JAMIE DAVIES	GBR	DALLARA F396 GM	15	27m 42.85s	102.35
12	MARTIN O'CONNELL	GBR	DALLARA F394 VAUXHALL	15	27m 55.69s	101.57
13	MARK SHAW	GBR	DALLARA F396 GM	15	27m 56.42s	101.53
14	SHINGO TACHI	JAP	DALLARA F394 TOYOTA	15	27m 57.80s	101.44
15	STEVE ARNOLD	GBR	DALLARA F396 MUGEN	15	27m 59.86s	101.32
16	KAZUTO YANAGAWA	JAP	TOM'S 036F TOYOTA	15	28m 07.50s	100.86
17	BEN COLLINS	GBR	DALLARA F394 MUGEN	15	28m 10.20s	100.70
18	MICHAEL BENTWOOD	GBR	DALLARA F394 MUGEN	15	28m 14.51s	100.44
19	PHILIP HOPKINS	GBR	DALLARA F394 FIAT	15	28m 14.90s	100.42
20	PAULA COOK	GBR	DALLARA F396 ALFA ROMEO	15	28m 17.79s	100.25
21	SIMON WILLS	NZ	DALLARA F394 VAUXHALL	15	28m 20.78s	100.07
R	TAKASHI YOKOYAMA	JAP	TOM'S 036F TOYOTA	10	ACCIDENT	
R	MARTIN BYFORD	GBR	DALLARA F396 OPEL	9	SUSPENSION	
R	ANGEL BURGUENO	SPA	DALLARA F396 OPEL	2	ACCIDENT	
FASTEST LAP	**JONNY KANE**				**1m 48.46s**	**104.62**

Firman, series leader • Smith and Montoya fight for position • Yokoyama takes to the grass

  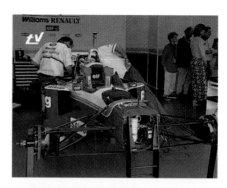

This year for the first time race-goers at the British Grand Prix were able to enjoy every second of the action, thanks to Silverstone TV.

Over three days we broadcast more than 40 hours of live TV featuring the famous names, the incidents and the excitement - on the track and off.

Visage Group would like to thank Silverstone Circuits Ltd. for their confidence and support in this unique venture and our 100 or so staff and freelancers who made Silverstone TV such a success.

Silverstone TV will be on the air again for Coys International Historic Festival (August 3rd-4th) and the ITC meeting (August 18th) - with an even bigger programme planned for next year.

VISAGE

Business Television   Facilities   Live Events   Multimedia

	PORSCHE SUPERCUP					
POSITION	DRIVER	NAT	CAR	LAPS	TIME/REASON	MPH
1	EMMANUEL COLLARD	FRA	PORSCHE 911 CUP 3.8	15	30m 35.463s	92.71
2	PATRICK HUISMAN	NED	PORSCHE 911 CUP 3.8	15	30m 40.636s	92.45
3	JÜRGEN VON GARTZEN	GER	PORSCHE 911 CUP 3.8	15	30m 46.988s	92.13
4	PATRICK SIMON	GER	PORSCHE 911 CUP 3.8	15	30m 51.127s	91.93
5	OLIVER MATHAI	GER	PORSCHE 911 CUP 3.8	15	30m 51.452s	91.91
6	DUNCAN HUISMAN	NED	PORSCHE 911 CUP 3.8	15	30m 56.200s	91.67
7	JORG BERGMEISTER	GER	PORSCHE 911 CUP 3.8	15	30m 58.188s	91.58
8	HORST FARNBACHER	GER	PORSCHE 911 CUP 3.8	15	30m 58.618s	91.55
9	HARALD GROHS	GER	PORSCHE 911 CUP 3.8	15	31m 00.829s	91.45
10	DANNY PFEIL	GER	PORSCHE 911 CUP 3.8	15	31m 02.243s	91.38
11	HANS WILLEMS	BEL	PORSCHE 911 CUP 3.8	15	31m 06.355s	91.18
12	JEAN-PIERRE MALCHER	FRA	PORSCHE 911 CUP 3.8	15	31m 11.227s	90.94
13	KEVIN SCHWANTZ	USA	PORSCHE 911 CUP 3.8	15	31m 12.774s	90.86
14	ANDREJ KULUNDZIC	YUG	PORSCHE 911 CUP 3.8	15	31m 15.568s	90.73
15	MATTEO MARIA GALIMBERTI	ITA	PORSCHE 911 CUP 3.8	15	31m 20.387s	90.49
16	JACQUES HEUCLIN	FRA	PORSCHE 911 CUP 3.8	15	31m 35.874s	89.76
17	MARC SCHOONBROODT	BEL	PORSCHE 911 CUP 3.8	15	31m 48.062s	89.18
18	CLAUDE-YVES GOSSELIN	FRA	PORSCHE 911 CUP 3.8	15	31m 55.004s	88.86
19	CHRISTOF VOGEL	GER	PORSCHE 911 CUP 3.8	15	31m 56.791s	88.78
20	MANUEL MONTEIRO	POR	PORSCHE 911 CUP 3.8	15	31m 58.934s	88.68
21	MICHEL MORA	FRA	PORSCHE 911 CUP 3.8	15	31m 59.152s	88.67
22	MARC ROSTAN	FRA	PORSCHE 911 CUP 3.8	15	31m 59.543s	88.65
23	HARALD BECKER	GER	PORSCHE 911 CUP 3.8	15	32m 17.846s	87.81
24	JEAN-LUC CHEREAU	FRA	PORSCHE 911 CUP 3.8	15	32m 26.613s	87.42
R	ALLAN McNISH	GBR	PORSCHE 911 CUP 3.8	14	SPIN	
R	JACK LECONTE	FRA	PORSCHE 911 CUP 3.8	13	MECHANICAL	
FASTEST LAP **Emmanuel Collard**					**2m 00.812s**	**93.90**

PHOTOGRAPH **JEFF BLOXHAM**

PHOTOGRAPH **GARY HAWKINS**

PHOTOGRAPH **JAKOB EBREY**

Grohs spins • McNish slithers into the gravel • Collard, easy winner

AN ELECTRONIC CANVAS FOR YOUR VIDEO IMAGES, STAFF MESSAGES, PROMOTIONAL AND ADVERTISING ACTIVITIES.

- Amazing clarity • Bright, stunning pictures • Potential revenue maker
- Flexible payment terms • Short & long term rental

FORMULA RENAULT EUROCUP

POSITION	DRIVER	NAT	CAR	LAPS	TIME	MPH
1	MARIO HABERFELD	BRA	VAN DIEMEN RF96 RENAULT	15	29m 22.22s	96.58
2	DAVID SAELENS	BEL	MYGALE FR96 RENAULT	15	29m 36.38s	95.81
3	DAVID HENDERSON	GBR	ERMOLI FR96 RENAULT	15	29m 38.82s	95.68
4	JEAN DE CASTELLI	FRA	MYGALE FR96 RENAULT	15	29m 42.66s	95.47
5	ETIENNE VAN DER LINDE	SAF	MARTINI MK72 RENAULT	15	29m 43.30s	95.44
6	DARREN TURNER	GBR	VAN DIEMEN RF96 RENAULT	15	29m 48.94s	95.14
7	OMAR GALEFFI	ITA	TATUUS RC96 RENAULT	15	29m 49.17s	95.13
8	DAVID COOK	GBR	TATUUS RC96 RENAULT	15	29m 50.01s	95.08
9	GIORGIO VINELLA	ITA	VAN DIEMEN RF96 RENAULT	15	29m 53.06s	94.92
10	JONATHAN TANDY	GBR	SWIFT SC95RS RENAULT	15	30m 28.65s	93.07
11	NASSIM SIDI SAID	ALG	MARTINI MK71/2 RENAULT	15	30m 34.99s	92.75
12	HEINRICH LANGFERMANN	GER	MYGALE FR96 RENAULT	15	31m 23.36s	90.37
13	MICHAEL NIPPERS	GBR	STRYX RT95B RENAULT	14	29m 40.85s	89.20
R	RODRIGO HANASHIRO	BRA	VAN DIEMEN RF96 RENAULT	9		
R	JEAN FIRINO MARTELL	FRA	MARTINI MK71 RENAULT	9		
R	DAVID ROBERTSON	GBR	ERMOLLI FR96 RENAULT	9		
R	JAMIE HUNTER	GBR	VAN DIEMEN RF96 RENAULT	7		
R	BRIAN SAUNDERS	GBR	MYGALE FR96 RENAULT	6		
R	ANGELO LANCELOTTI	ITA	TATUUS RC96 RENAULT	6		
R	ALEXANDER YOONG	MAL	MYGALE FR96 RENAULT	6		
R	CLAUDE DEGREMONT	FRA	MYGALE FR96 RENAULT	6		
R	ENRIQUE BERNOLDI	BRA	TATUUS RC96 RENAULT	2		
R	HOOVER ORSI	BRA	VAN DIEMEN RF96 RENAULT	1		
R	HANS PETER SUNDBERG	SWE	TATUUS RC96 RENAULT	1		
R	JIRI DE VIERMAN	BEL	VAN DIEMEN RF96 RENAULT	0		
R	PAOLO MACCARI	ITA	TATUUS RC96 RENAULT	0		
R	CHRISTIAN VANN	GBR	VAN DIEMEN RF96 RENAULT	0		
R	ROLLO McNALLY	GBR	VAN DIEMEN RF96 RENAULT	0		
R	TIM SPOUGE	GBR	TATUUS RC96 RENAULT	0		
R	TOR SRIACHAVONON	THA	TATUUS RC96 RENAULT	0		
EXC	ANDREA DE LORENZI	ITA	TATUUS RC96 RENAULT	15	29m 45.76s	95.31
FASTEST LAP	**MARIO HABERFELD**				**1m 56.54s**	**97.36**

UNISYS

PHOTOGRAPH **SUTTON MOTORSPORT IMAGES**

PHOTOGRAPH **JEFF BLOXHAM**

To the limits!

	DUNLOP ROVER TURBO CUP					
POSITION	DRIVER	NAT	CAR	LAPS	TIME/REASON	MPH
1	ALASTAIR LYALL	GBR	ROVER 220 COUPE	12	27m 04.761s	83.80
2	JEREMY COTTERILL	GBR	ROVER 220 COUPE	12	27m 11.615s	83.45
3	RICHARD DEAN	GBR	ROVER 220 COUPE	12	27m 16.205s	83.22
4	STEPHEN DAY	GBR	ROVER 220 COUPE	12	27m 19.838s	83.03
5	PIERS JOHNSON	GBR	ROVER 220 COUPE	12	27m 21.739s	82.94
6	NICK CARR	GBR	ROVER 220 COUPE	12	27m 22.526s	82.90
7	JOHN LLEWELLYN	GBR	ROVER 220 COUPE	12	27m 24.055s	82.82
8	NIGEL EDWARDS	GBR	ROVER 220 COUPE	12	27m 24.841s	82.78
9	ANDY ACKERLEY	GBR	ROVER 220 COUPE	12	27m 26.085s	82.72
10	IAN SUMMERFIELD	GBR	ROVER 220 COUPE	12	27m 26.505s	82.70
11	PHILIP VERELLEN	BEL	ROVER 220 COUPE	12	27m 28.387s	82.60
12	BRIAN HEEREY	GBR	ROVER 220 COUPE	12	27m 33.142s	82.36
13	DAVE COLE	GBR	ROVER 220 COUPE	12	27m 44.112s	81.82
14	RUSSELL GRADY	GBR	ROVER 220 COUPE	12	27m 44.677s	81.79
15	ANDREW BRAKEWELL	GBR	ROVER 220 COUPE	12	27m 47.099s	81.67
16	VINCE MARTIN	GBR	ROVER 220 COUPE	12	27m 58.408s	81.12
17	NICK JAMES	GBR	ROVER 220 COUPE	12	27m 58.738s	81.11
18	MIKE BULMER	GBR	ROVER 220 COUPE	12	28m 01.228s	80.99
19	IAN GRISWOLD	GBR	ROVER 220 COUPE	12	28m 01.969s	80.95
20	RICHARD HANN	GBR	ROVER 220 COUPE	11	27m 29.650s	75.66
21	PHILIP BURGESS	GBR	ROVER 220 COUPE	11	28m 02.468s	74.18
R	LAURENCE PLUMMER	GBR	ROVER 220 COUPE	11	TRANSMISSION	
R	JAMIE WALL	GBR	ROVER 220 COUPE	0	ACCIDENT	
R	MARTIN JOBLING	GBR	ROVER 220 COUPE	0	ACCIDENT	
EXC	EUGENE O'BRIEN	GBR	ROVER 220 COUPE	12	27m 15.067s	83.27
EXC	MARK HAZELL	GBR	ROVER 220 COUPE	12	27m 43.600s	81.85
FASTEST LAP	RICHARD DEAN				2m 14.131s	84.59

UNISYS

PHOTOGRAPH **SUTTON MOTORSPORT IMAGES**   PHOTOGRAPH **RALPH HARDWICK**   PHOTOGRAPH **JOHN COLLEY**

Chase the ace • Comfortable winner Alastair Lyall • Unlucky 13 – O'Brien in the gravel

Team Work

The Formula for Success

At Hewlett-Packard we recognise that to deliver a Grand Prix quality computing capability to our customers we must develop a strong team spirit with them. We understand the need to rapidly respond to requests for help, with a fast and accurate solution every time. It's a relationship that we've developed with Jordan Grand Prix as their technical sponsors. Our Team Work strategy is helping us to get closer to our customers and helping to promote them to the pole position of their own leagues.

To find out more about Team Work with Hewlett-Packard Service & Support

call 01344 361386

Hewlett-Packard are technical sponsors to Jordan Grand Prix

	RENAULT SPORT SPIDER ELF TROPHY					
POSITION	**DRIVER**	**NAT**	**CAR**	**LAPS**	**TIME**	**MPH**
1	JASON PLATO	GBR	RENAULT SPORT SPIDER	15	32m 19.05s	87.77
2	FRANCK LAGORCE	FRA	RENAULT SPORT SPIDER	15	32m 23.63s	87.57
3	JULIAN WESTWOOD	GBR	RENAULT SPORT SPIDER	15	32m 23.83s	87.56
4	SCOTT LAKIN	GBR	RENAULT SPORT SPIDER	15	32m 26.97s	87.42
5	MAGNUS WALLINDER	SWE	RENAULT SPORT SPIDER	15	32m 27.93s	87.37
6	JAN NILSSON	SWE	RENAULT SPORT SPIDER	15	32m 29.81s	87.29
7	JEAN-PHILIPPE HAOUZA	FRA	RENAULT SPORT SPIDER	15	32m 40.20s	86.83
8	JOSE JOAO MAGALHAES	POR	RENAULT SPORT SPIDER	15	32m 40.62s	86.81
9	XAVIER LANGLOIS	FRA	RENAULT SPORT SPIDER	15	32m 42.04s	86.75
10	JACOB SUND	DEN	RENAULT SPORT SPIDER	15	32m 42.96s	86.70
11	BERNARD THUNER	SWI	RENAULT SPORT SPIDER	15	32m 47.84s	86.49
12	JEAN-CHRISTOPHE BOULLION	FRA	RENAULT SPORT SPIDER	15	32m 48.17s	86.48
13	MARCEL KLAEY	SWI	RENAULT SPORT SPIDER	15	32m 49.66s	86.41
14	RALPH DRUCKENMULLER	GER	RENAULT SPORT SPIDER	15	32m 50.52s	86.37
15	PIERRE DE THOISY	FRA	RENAULT SPORT SPIDER	15	32m 53.91s	86.22
16	DONALD MOLENAAR	NED	RENAULT SPORT SPIDER	15	33m 00.71s	85.93
17	MICHAEL BLEEKEMOLEN	NED	RENAULT SPORT SPIDER	15	33m 07.16s	85.65
18	ALESSANDRO SEBASTI SCALERA	ITA	RENAULT SPORT SPIDER	15	33m 07.58s	85.63
19	PIM VAN RIET	NED	RENAULT SPORT SPIDER	15	33m 10.05s	85.52
20	BERNARD CASTAGNE	FRA	RENAULT SPORT SPIDER	15	33m 13.00s	85.40
21	PIERRE CORTHALS	BEL	RENAULT SPORT SPIDER	15	33m 13.75s	85.37
22	TOBIAS SCHLESINGER	GER	RENAULT SPORT SPIDER	15	33m 16.62s	85.24
23	CLAUDIO BURLOTTI	ITA	RENAULT SPORT SPIDER	15	33m 41.83s	84.18
24	OLIVER FREYMUTH	GER	RENAULT SPORT SPIDER	15	33m 42.31s	84.16
25	DENIS GIBAUD	FRA	RENAULT SPORT SPIDER	15	33m 42.51s	84.15
26	PETER VAN MERKSTEIJN	NED	RENAULT SPORT SPIDER	15	33m 50.81s	83.81
27	FRANCIS MAILLET	FRA	RENAULT SPORT SPIDER	15	33m 59.99s	83.43
28	MAURO SERRA	BRA	RENAULT SPORT SPIDER	15	34m 02.69s	83.32
29	FRANCO CARUSO	ITA	RENAULT SPORT SPIDER	15	34m 05.06s	83.22
R	ERIK VAN VLIET	NED	RENAULT SPORT SPIDER	11		
R	ALAIN GIRADET	SWI	RENAULT SPORT SPIDER	10		
R	DAVID SHAW	GBR	RENAULT SPORT SPIDER	8		
R	RUPERT HOFMARCHER	AUT	RENAULT SPORT SPIDER	6		
R	SEAN McNALLY	GBR	RENAULT SPORT SPIDER	6		
R	ENRIQUE BERNOLDI	BRA	RENAULT SPORT SPIDER	5		
R	JEAN PIERRE PLA	FRA	RENAULT SPORT SPIDER	3		
FASTEST LAP	**JASON PLATO & JEAN-CHRISTOPHE BOULLION**				**2m 08.10s**	**88.58**

UNISYS

Getting the shot. The F1 photographers in position

PHOTOGRAPH **SUTTON MOTORSPORT IMAGES**

SUTTON MOTORSPORT IMAGES
left to right, back row **Neil Hepworth, Mark Sutton, Keith Sutton, Paul Sutton, Staurt Collins** left to right, front row **Gavin Lawrence, Mark Leader, Alex Littlewood, Mike Weston**

PHOTOGRAPH **RALPH HARDWICK**

AUTOSPORT PHOTOGRAPHIC
left to right:
Ralph Hardwick, Martyn Elford, Jeff Bloxham

PHOTOGRAPH **TIM WRIGHT**

The terraces are empty, and the crowd on its way home after the 1996 British Grand Prix at Silverstone.
All that's left is the debris, which is quickly cleared up by the volunteer litter patrols.

Parting shot

PHOTOGRAPH **RALPH HARDWICK**